EBURY PRESS
HOW TO RAISE A PLANT BABY

Vinayak Garg is the founder of Lazy Gardener, a company and community that has inspired thousands of Indians and people around the world to take up home gardening. He was named 2021 Entrepreneur 35 Under 35 and Sustainability Hero of 2020 by *The Better India*. Vinayak completed his engineering from Indian Institute of Technology Delhi. His email address is vinayak@vinayakgarg.com.

ADVANCE PRAISE FOR THE BOOK

'My mom is the happy gardener in my house and she is always complaining to the gardener that her plants are not getting enough nutrition. And he is the ultimate "lazy gardener" . . . he tries to do the least possible! So I'm sure she'd love the plant food sticks to use in our garden . . . I've been noting through your posts how they seem to be a blessing for plants. As the title suggests, Vinayak Garg's *How to Raise a Plant Baby* gives readers easy tips and tricks about growing healthy plants that are best suited for urban settings'—Archana Puran Singh, Indian actor and television personality

'Vinayak is just amazing and so passionate, everything he does is inspiring! I am also learning and growing and applying. My mom is the real greenskeeper whose plants are her babies, and I am just in awe of how she takes care of them. Vinayak Garg has written a must-read primer for anyone considering gardening. Read this book and learn from one of the absolute best'—Prachi Desai, Indian film actor

'This gardening book is not only great to look at, it tells you everything you need to know to grow and sustain happy plants. Vinayak, through his experience, shares his story of maintaining his own garden. This book is ideal for beginners as well as pro gardeners'—Divyanka Tripathi, Indian television actor

'You don't always need a bungalow with a garden to indulge your love for gardening. From the magnetic planters for the fridge to the test tubes . . . one can have greenery around them however and wherever they want. To see the steady growth of Lazy Gardener has been wonderful. He has packed all his knowledge into his book; Vinayak shares various methods with all of us to take better care of our houseplants' —Sumona Chakravarti, Indian film and television actor

'Vinayak is empowering people to take up gardening. The book not only explores what gardening is in a practical sense but also what it means to each of us: an opportunity for connecting with nature and a practice that is always evolving'—Vani Murthy, TEDx speaker, composting enthusiast and urban farmer (IG: @wormrani)

'I've been a nature lover and an avid gardener my whole life, and so was delighted with Vinayak's story of his experiences with gardening. Vinayak is empowering people to take up gardening. A great read and a true gem of information on gardening'—Vidya Malavade, Indian film actor and yoga teacher

'As a novice gardener, I have been keeping houseplants for a very long time, but I've still learned new things from Vinayak and this book. The book is also for experienced gardeners and beginners who are fed up of losing plants'—Shwetambari Shetty, fitness expert at Cure.Fit, co-founder of The Tribe-Fitness Club

'Gardening, just like reading, is a hobby that helps one forget their troubles and immerse themselves in doing something productive. As you lose yourself in nature, you observe and learn new things—about the world and yourself. Whether you are already a proud plant parent or trying to get into the hobby, this book will inspire you to hone your gardening skills'—Aakriti Ahuja, Indian entrepreneur, actor, radio jockey and television presenter

'In today's generation while we see the youngsters being so irresponsible and not bothered about soil exhaustion and about trees being cut, it's nice to see Vinayak being so hyperactively involved in spreading the message of growing plants'—Sanjjanaa Galrani, south Indian film actor and philanthropist

'Gardening couldn't have been made easier for people with busy lives like me. This book is amazing and it tells you everything you need to know to grow happy plants. Vinayak, through his wisdom and experience, shares his story of maintaining his own garden. This book is ideal for all'—Sushruthi Krishna, entrepreneur, founder of Saaki, and former Miss India runner-up

'Gardening is a learning process, and with so many sources of information to help and guide you, it can be hard to know how to begin or where to look to learn more. In his book, Vinayak has provided step-by-step gardening guides in an easy-to-understand manner'—Reena Kapoor, Indian film and television actor

'I had come across Vinayak from Lazy Gardener's Instagram handle and YouTube channel, and I learnt a lot about urban gardening in just a couple of videos and educational posts. Vinayak has a lovely, straightforward style so this will appeal to amateurs as well'—Malini Kapoor, Indian television and theatre actor

'This book is perfect. You don't need to be a new plant parent either; if you have plants and you want to keep them alive and know what you're doing and how to troubleshoot, get this book'—Manasi Moghe, Indian actor, artist and model

'Thanks to Vinayak, I was able to start my successful journey into gardening. Vinayak has done an excellent job of penning down the advice in a structured manner for anyone who is considering gardening'—Nilu Kohli, Indian film and television actor

'A must-have for plants, planting and gardens. If you are a plant parent and have a question, this book will have the answer. Every gardener needs this encyclopaedic guide to gardening'—Harsh Dixit, celebrity go-to chef for many celebrities in India

'*How to Raise a Plant Baby* is a great book, it tells one everything they need to know to grow and sustain happy plants. Vinayak shares his story of maintaining his own garden. This book is perfect for beginners as well as pro gardeners'—Amninder Sandhu, award-winning chef at Arth and A Bar Called Life

'Urban gardeners, who are short of space and time, would like to check out this book'—Pavitra Punia, Indian actor and entrepreneur

'This is a wonderful garden resource, not assuming whether you are new to gardening or not. If I could only have three books about gardening, this would be on top of my list. This is one of those books that you keep open on your counter throughout the seasons of gardening, because it's that helpful'—Aadi, radio jockey, YouTuber and entertainer

'Ghar Kheti was an amazing initiative I took on radio during lockdown, where I encouraged people to grow vegetables at home on their own. In this journey, I got in touch with Lazy Gardener, Vinayak Garg. What a journey we have had together while boosting people to grow at home. And now you are putting your gardening journey here in this book, it will be a great read and true gem of information on gardening for all the readers . . . #HappyGharKiKheti with #LazyGardener guys'—Ravi Gurjar, programming director at Radio City 91.1, Delhi

'This warm, wonderful and inspiring book shows you how to raise happy, healthy plants forever'—Pratiksha, radio jockey at 94.3 My FM, Surat

'I initially engaged with Vinayak in the creation of Delhi's first man-made forest in January 2020. I am delighted with Vinayak's story of his experiences with gardening. This book is a great read'—Manav, anchor and producer, Zee Media Corporation, and former radio jockey at Radio City

'Vinayak is encouraging everyone to take up gardening. The book explores what gardening is in a practical sense and is an opportunity for us to connect with nature'—Ishita Sudha Yashvi, entrepreneur, mar-com specialist and content creator (IG: @ishitasudhayashvi)

How to Raise a Plant Baby

A BEGINNER'S GUIDE
TO HAPPY PLANTS

VINAYAK GARG
Founder *of* LAZY GARDENER

EBURY
PRESS

An imprint of Penguin Random House

EBURY PRESS

USA | Canada | UK | Ireland | Australia
New Zealand | India | South Africa | China

Ebury Press is part of the Penguin Random House group of companies
whose addresses can be found at global.penguinrandomhouse.com

Published by Penguin Random House India Pvt. Ltd
4th Floor, Capital Tower 1, MG Road,
Gurugram 122 002, Haryana, India

First published in Ebury Press by Penguin Random House India 2022

Illustrations by Tejas Modak

ISBN 9780143455110

Typeset in Adobe Garamond Pro by Manipal Technologies Limited, Manipal
Printed at Thomson Press India Ltd, New Delhi

www.penguin.co.in

To Mili,
the future gardeners of the world,
and anyone who has ever had a plant die on them

Contents

Part III: Ongoing Care for Your Plant

Foreword

Like many others, I greatly enjoy nature. I clearly recall the delight I felt as a young man in Tibet during my travels outside Lhasa, in seeing the variety of flora and fauna that thrived in my country. Here in India, I have enjoyed walking up the mountains above my home in Dharamsala, where I had admired the various types of trees and plants. I have also learned much about nature and its need to be cared for from tending my own small garden.

Our ancestors viewed the earth as rich and bountiful, many considering nature to be inexhaustibly sustainable. We know now that for the environment upon which we depend for our nourishment and survival to endure, we must care for it. In the past, our lack of care for Mother Nature might have resulted from ignorance. However, with the information we possess today, it is essential that we re-examine our attitudes toward the precious gift we have inherited and for which we are responsible, in order for it to be enjoyed by future generations.

In his book on gardening, Vinayak shares his experiences, highlighting his delight in caring for flowers and plants. I hope it will encourage others to appreciate nature and strive to sustain our only home for the coming generations to enjoy.

His Holiness The Dalai Lama
20 April 2022

Part I

The Growth of a Gardener

'The creation of a thousand forests is in one acorn.'
—*Ralph Waldo Emerson*

My life is rooted in plants. They are an extension of my family. Growing up, my family would spend time together taking care of plants. Every evening, we would relax on our balcony in the company of our green friends. We spent our weekends gardening, and I have many fond memories of my sister Keerti and I playing outdoors, laughing and spraying plants (and sometimes one another) with the gardening hose. My mother took dozens of pictures of Keerti and I, carefully placing tall, bushy money plants snaking up moss sticks on either side of us. While my mother didn't go out of her way to grow plants from seeds or formally study gardening, she knew a lot about plants and taught Keerti and I everything she knew. She taught us the botanical names of plants, how to pay attention to their needs and how to 'steal' a plant cutting and grow a full plant from it.

A madhumalti creeper crawling it's way up to the roof at my home

On the facade of our home grew a madhumalti creeper (Rangoon creeper) that crawled its way up to the roof. Year-round, it would flower and produce small round black seeds. Keerti and I both enjoyed collecting these seeds, drying them in the sun and storing them in jars and soap boxes in the cupboard. Whenever our friends and family visited and appreciated the creeper, we would hand them some seeds and say, 'Look, you can grow one too!'

Outside our house was a five-by-ten-foot patch where we grew a small collection of plants that were useful in some way, such as mehndi plants for making henna and curry leaves for cooking. The mehndi plant also served as a hedge between that area and the walkways around our home. My mother liked to give curry leaves to her friends as a gift, especially if they enjoyed cooking. My father likes to reminisce about the neighbours and vegetable vendors who would come to pick cuttings of both the mehndi and curry leaf plants. Before commercial nurseries became popular, people simply traded cuttings with their friends and neighbours. Someone would walk up and say, ' I use this for cooking. I don't have a plant at home. Can I take this?' Sometimes it was neighbours, other times it was the vegetable vendors who drove through various neighbourhoods making a living selling vegetables. Whenever we trimmed the mehndi hedge, my father would put a heap of cuttings outside for the vendors. I still like to share the joy of plants by giving seeds or cuttings to my friends or anyone else who is interested.

My mother once took a week-long course on how to graft cacti, which is a technique for growing different types of cacti on top of each other to get a unique-looking cactus. Cacti are easy plants to maintain and graft, so it was a fun and simple method for me to grasp as a young child. I went along with her, and we learnt how to graft cacti together.

My school, Sardar Patel Vidyalaya, also taught me to care for plants. Whenever the teachers or faculty wanted to close off an area to students, they wouldn't do so with a fence or a gate, but with a row of potted plants. There were marigolds and salvia in front of the principal's office, for example, to give the principal more privacy. We were told not to run around the potted plants and to be careful, that 'if the plant falls, it will get hurt'. We were taught to honour plants and their space. The school had a canteen courtyard with large mulberry and neem trees in the middle of it that provided us with shade as we held assemblies and ate our rice and sambhar or idli or sabji and roti. As curious children, we would wonder, 'How did this tree get here in the middle of my building?' The teachers would tell us that the tree was there first. The building came later.

We used to have our morning assemblies outside in an open field under a sheesham (rosewood) tree. Its wide branches and foliage would provide us with cool shade. The teachers would even pause in their lessons from time to time so that we could simply observe the tree. They would tell us that the tree and its leaves signalled the change of seasons. At the start of the school year, our teachers would remind us, 'A few months ago, this tree had no leaves, but if you look now, it has sprouted many new ones. Your previous school year and exam scores are in the past. Just like this tree, you have a fresh start. This is a new class. We will do something new.'

The plants and trees around Sardar Patel Vidyalaya were also our sturdy, reliable playmates. The playground was designed around the trees and the mud hill they grew out of. On either side of the trees were sloping ramps that we enjoyed running up and down. Between the trees was a large concrete tunnel. We would hide in this tunnel to surprise one another or to admire nature in solitude.

In February and March, when the mulberry and jamun trees bore fruit, the older children would shake the trees while the younger kids would laugh and run around to pick the fruit up off the ground. Some were sour and green, while others were dark red and sweet. We would trade the different coloured berries. Kids would convince each other that the ripe blue-black ones were better than the unripe green ones, or that the pink and red jamun berries tasted the best. Someone might say, 'Oh, I want to take some home for my brother, but I only want the black ones,' to which their friend might say, 'Take my black ones and give me those green ones.'

In the summer, Keerti and I would visit our *mamaji* and *mamiji* in Meerut or our *bua* and *fufaji* in Rohtak. They were both professors and lived on a university campus. They had lawns surrounding their home. You would see many people gardening.

They would typically grow plants that served their daily needs. Even people who weren't into gardening would have four or five guava or lemon trees around their house. Their philosophy was to have fruit to trade. They would either grow trees that produced a lot of fruit or grow fruit that they didn't eat a lot of. My mamaji had many lemon trees, so he would trade lemons with his neighbours for other fruit and herbs. Before that, I had only seen fruit in the market, so these summer trips are some of my earliest memories of seeing fruit come off the tree.

My mamiji grew roses to place in vases around their home, especially in areas where she prayed. Every night, she would place a bowl filled with freshly plucked raat ki rani (night flowering jasmine) next to our bed, so that the sweet fragrance filled the room. Whenever we visited, our mamaji and mamiji would show us how different trees had grown. They had kathal trees with giant, spiky green fruit stuck to the trunk, which mystified Keerti and me. There were also neem trees that could be used for medicine and a natural pesticide to keep insects away from other plants. The banyan trees fascinated us the most; their roots dangled down from the branches and stabbed through the ground like many little tree trunks. We would soak banyan leaves in water and then scrape the chlorophyll off with a toothbrush to expose their delicate, lace-like venation, then we would use these leaves for crafts or to adorn idols. Keerti and I, along with our parents, would also arrange banyan leaves like puzzle pieces to create animal shapes.

When we saw a tree we didn't recognize, Keerti and I would ask many questions: 'How old is that tree? Who planted it? Did it, too, come from a seed?' When Keerti and I learnt that some of the trees were forty, fifty or a hundred years old, we truly appreciated not only the wonders of nature but also the value of time.

Yet, in far less time than it took for some of my mamaji's trees to grow to their present height, I have seen roads, buildings and cars take space away from nature. My parents planted a small ficus plant near their new home right after they got married, a few years before I was born. Today, it is around fifty feet tall. At the time they planted it, it was all right for people to take care of public spaces and contribute their own plants. Now, if somebody does that, it is seen as reducing the number of parking spots. I have witnessed disputes over whether plants or a car have the right to a patch of land. It feels like the lessons that my teachers taught me about coexisting with nature are being forgotten.

By the time I was a teenager, much of the green space in our neighbourhood had been paved over to make way for parking spaces, wider roads and drainage systems. High rises began blocking the sunlight that shone down on our balcony and outdoor garden. The five-by-ten-foot patch where we grew plants became another place to put a vehicle. Neighbours came by less and less to collect clippings. The curry and mehndi plants that once lined the streets were replaced by Maruti 800s.

To keep up with the growing infrastructure, my family decided to expand our home. Towards the end of my primary schooling, we added an extra storey to our house, but in return, we lost our dear madhumalti creeper. My father believes it died because the painters dumped toxic wastewater on it, but it may have also suffered due to the construction of the neighbourhood drainage system. Although we lost the creeper, the renovations gave my parents more space to grow plants on the balcony. During the original build, my father had put recesses in the brick railing of the balcony to hold soil where we could grow small flowers and vines. He created even more of these recesses in the extension. My father also made sure that the builders installed iron rods along the roof for hanging plants. They even recreated the Mughal entrance from a mould they had kept of the original design of the house with the intention of adorning the entrance with plants.

I was excited to see more plants around our family home! However, this was around the time I left home for college. I was accepted at IIT Delhi, where I studied engineering. I stayed in a hostel, practically living out of my suitcase. My time at IIT Delhi went by in a blur. When I wasn't in class, taking exams in the lab or studying, I would be participating in Baja competitions run by the Society of Automotive Engineers, building and racing small off-road vehicles against other teams. I even spent a year as an exchange student in Lyon, France. Plants were not really in the picture.

After I graduated from college, I had a chance to settle my busy mind. I was among twelve fellows chosen under the Gurukul programme run by the Foundation for Universal Responsibility of His Holiness Dalai Lama. The Gurukul programme was a structured stay in the monastery of H.H. Dalai Lama at McLeod Ganj with an introduction to Buddhism and a window into Tibetan culture. I spent two months maintaining the monastery, preparing food and gardening. It was there that I was reminded of the joy that gardening brought to my life. When you work in a monastery, you are focused on your task rather than letting your mind wander. You are present. Instead of thinking about your next meeting, what to buy or where you want to go next in life, you just are. By being present in this way, I was reminded of what mattered to me the most: nature.

But that reminder quickly slipped away as I stepped back into routine life. Like many recent college graduates, I dove into corporate culture. I accepted a job at a large multinational corporation focused on energy reform. Then I launched an education company. Two years after that, I started another company focused on digital healthcare. Everything was on the move. I was constantly uprooted, like a plant being relocated from one pot to another.

Throughout my college years and the time I spent working my way up the corporate ladder, I would occasionally visit my family home. I noticed that my parents still took care of plants, but they had yet to touch the recesses and rods that they had added when the extension was built. My mother has a theory about taking care of plants: only place plants in areas that you frequent. She often waters plants and checks on them when she's talking on the phone or taking care of some household task. Going out of her way to take care of a plant is a big ask, and she hardly ever went up to the second floor.

Four years out of college, I moved back home, but the recesses were still plant-less. I was working on my new business from the second floor of my childhood home, but all the plants were on the first floor. I had this big balcony with a lot of space that got plenty of light but nothing growing on it. It went on like that for a while, me upstairs working on my business and the plants downstairs where my parents were. Once my business got going and I had a team to help and more time on my hands, I finally decided to add some plants upstairs.

I bought four huge pots without knowing how I would get them upstairs. I carried one up by myself, but two months later, the other three were still on the first floor. Eventually, I hired someone to bring them upstairs. They don't call me the 'lazy gardener' for nothing.

Once the pots were upstairs, I planted a *champa* (plumeria) plant, a lemon tree, a papaya tree and a fig tree, then positioned them on the balcony so they got the light they needed. Because of the development around my parents' home, tall towers blocked sunlight from reaching the lower floors. If I wanted my plants to get bright light, I had to place them somewhere on the second floor or higher.

I was interested in growing food, so I read about which food I could grow without attracting bugs. Bugs make gardening a lot less relaxing. Gardening is supposed to be an activity that you can do at your own leisure. But whenever bugs show up, I have to go into crisis mode, moving plants around, changing pots and soil as fast as I can to save my plants. I ended up growing spinach and coriander because they're not as popular with the creepy-crawly crowd. Then I experimented with bell pepper and ladies' fingers. My workspace finally looked lush and green. I had fruit, vegetables and herbs growing outside. I could breathe better. I felt much happier. Today, this balcony is where my parents enjoy their tea surrounded by lemon trees, fig trees, tomatoes and papaya.

Around the time I enlivened my workspace with plants, I found myself joining other people in my society to save a local park. Shiva Vatika Park is home to hundreds of trees and plants, including eucalyptus trees, Ashoka trees, mehndi shrubs, sadabahar (periwinkle) plants and a sheesham tree. Many generations of children and families gather there to play, practise karate and yoga, and spend quality time.

Across the street was a local market with several grocery stores, sweet shops and bakeries. Over time, more and more people started driving to the market instead of walking, jamming up the roads. City planners developed a twenty-year plan that proposed turning the park into a parking garage.

At first, they tried to appease the nature advocates by adding a lawn on top of the garage. The problem was that the lawn would be made up of grass and flowers, not deep-rooted trees. In fact, a park with trees is easier to maintain than a lawn, which requires constant watering and landscaping. Trees and shrubs can be sustained on groundwater while lawns typically require an entire watering system so that the grass doesn't dry up. The lawn would have been an irresponsible and unsustainable replacement for the park, where trees had grown for decades. I understand that cities need to grow so people can move in to pursue opportunities and chase their dreams, but we don't need to fight against nature. We just need better planning.

A movement grew overnight to save the park. Around 250 of my neighbours came together as a show of strength to protect the park as a bedrock of the community. We sent letters to counsellors, members of the legislative assembly, state government officials and regional newspapers advocating for the preservation of Shiva Vatika Park. We even got architects to weigh in on why the space could not be recreated on shallow soil laid on top of the parking garage. After a two-month fight, we won. Instead of building a parking garage, the city created a U-turn area so that there was more space for people to drive around as they searched for street parking. Just as I had learnt in school, trees had the first right to the land. The park was saved.

A couple of years later, our family sprouted a new generation; Keerti had a baby girl, Mili, and I officially became Mama Vinayak. I was excited for my sister to be a mother, and for the opportunity to show Mili the important things in life, such as how to be mindful of her surroundings, make new friends and shake a jamun tree to make the berries fall to the ground.

I was curious what colour berry would be her favourite. I flew to California to meet my new niece and catch up with my sister.

As Keerti and I talked during my first night there, we travelled through our childhood memories: going out into nature every weekend, where we would garden and play in the water; waiting for our mother to grab the money plants every time we took a photo together; watching our father give cuttings to neighbours and vendors; and collecting the seeds of our madhumalti creeper to give to family and friends. The memories were supposed to make us happy, but they were bittersweet. Keerti pointed out that there was less green space than there used to be. She didn't have as much time to focus on gardening because she had a job, and now she had Mili to nurture too. Plants had been a big part of our childhood; but would they be a big part of my niece's?

Would Mili learn that plants had the first right to the land as they did at Sardar Patel Vidyalaya and Shiva Vatika Park, or would she see vehicles as the rightful heirs to the space around us?

Would she have the opportunity to share seeds with her friends and cuttings with her neighbours so they could grow something they didn't have, or would she only buy fruit and vegetables at the market?

Would she grow up around parks with deep-rooted trees or only around lawns on top of parking garages?

Would she learn to garden and grow her own plants?

I realized that I could play a role in helping Mili embrace plants. Although there wasn't much space and Keerti had limited time, I could still show Mili how to garden and grow in low-light spaces in a way that didn't require too much of Keerti's time. So, on her birthday, I gave Mili a gardening kit, and we now make memories in the garden together, much like my parents did with Keerti and I.

Mili picking up a lemon with the lemon tree behind her and a lot of fallen lemons on the grass

As Mili has grown, so have her plants. She now has a lemon tree that she adores. She's not yet tall enough to pick lemons from the branches, so she gets excited when she sees ripe lemons that have fallen to the ground. She toddles over, picks them up, shows them to her mother and drops them into her special lemon bucket.

One day, Mili will no longer toddle and will be tall enough to pick the lemons off her tree rather than wait for them to fall. As she grows, she will become more aware of challenges that are far more complex than being too short to pick lemons. I know that the same issues that started with my generation and the generations before me—taking nature for granted, overdevelopment and climate change—will haunt Mili's generation and cascade into even greater challenges.

The first step that we can all take to address these challenges is to inspire ourselves and others to stay connected to nature by learning to care for plants. A single plant can't change the world, but a single gardener can.

This book is for everyone who, like my niece, is just getting into gardening.

I want to help you find the plant that's right for you and teach you how to grow happy, healthy plants no matter where you live.

I want to give you the confidence to start growing plants at home.

I want to show you how becoming a plant parent can benefit your well-being and the well-being of others.

I want to connect you with gardeners throughout India and around the world to exchange ideas much like my family and our neighbours' exchanged cuttings.

Most of all, I want you to know that anyone can grow their own plants.

It all starts with a seed.

1

Why Get into Gardening

It can sometimes seem like there are a million things fighting for our attention: the news, our jobs, the people in our lives, our favourite television shows, new things to learn, relaxation, exercise, hobbies . . . It often feels like there isn't enough time to do everything we want or need to do. What I love about plants is that they fit naturally into our lives. Plants are not only a great hobby, but they are also our companions. We can share plants with the people in our lives. Plants teach us new things and help us relax. And if you have a plant in a giant pot like I did and decide to move it yourself, gardening can be a good workout, too!

Gardening can fit into any lifestyle. Even if you have only ten minutes in your busy day, that's still plenty of time to check on a plant. Just like my mother was able to find the time to spend with her plants while doing other mundane tasks around the house, you too can steal a few peaceful moments to enjoy with your plant babies.

If you still need convincing that gardening is worth your time, let's explore several of the ways that plants improve our lives. And if you're already convinced, you should still keep reading. When we take the time to note all the benefits of gardening, our heart fills up.

Plants make us happy

There is a feeling of serenity we all get when we're surrounded by greenery, whether we're in a forest, a field of flowers, a greenhouse, a garden, or even inside a room or hallway lined with plants. We feel calmer and less on edge. Our feelings go to a more natural place. We are more aware that we are a part of nature.

Plants show us the passage of time so we can better observe change. One of the great joys of having a plant is seeing what has changed since yesterday and wondering what will change by tomorrow. Will the leaves grow? Will there be a new split in the branches? Will it start to flower or produce new fruit? When we see new growth and another day of happiness for our plants, we observe a small win for the plant, which becomes a small win for us as well. These small daily successes reassure us, brightening our mood.

The blissful feeling we get from plants isn't just in our imagination. Research has conclusively shown that spending time with plants calms our nervous system and lowers our blood pressure. Beginning in 2019, the United Kingdom's National Health Service started to prescribe plants to patients with anxiety and depression. While some people prefer a support dog or cat, pets can be hard to take care of. For others, it is simply best to be with their plants.

Because plants grow at a slow pace, they are relatively consistent compared to other things in our lives. They stabilize us emotionally, giving us a sense of purpose without an overwhelming amount of responsibility. Plants are an anchor in one's life. I've received numerous testimonials from the Lazy Gardener community about how plants have helped them improve their mental health and work through difficult circumstances. Plants have helped many people process grief, feel less alone and overcome anxiety and depression.

Over the years, I have gathered stories from friends, family and acquaintances about the impact plants have had on their lives. These stories teach and inspire others to adopt plants. You can read about some of these experiences in the final chapter of this book. If you have a story of your own that you would like to share, I would love to hear it! Email me at plantstories@lazygardener.in

Plants look amazing

Think back to when you were a kid and you saw a big tree and wanted to climb it. What made you want to climb it? The texture of the bark, perfect to grip with your feet and your hands? A low-hanging limb that looked like a giant arm, waiting to scoop you up? The branches that were spaced out just right for you and your friends to grab on to? The foliage, and wondering what it would look like when you climbed deep into the branches and were surrounded by a sea of colourful leaves? Trees are a natural playground that we see and immediately want to play on because of how they look.

Plants brighten our surroundings and our day. When I walk to the park near my home in New Delhi, I marvel at the buildings and all the signs of human civilization, but my attention always comes back to the green spaces that persevere:

the plants that break their way through the footpaths; the bushes and bougainvillea that fill the road medians; and the vertical gardens on the metro pillars. These plants make the city look less mechanical and more natural, creating a sense of calm amidst the hustle and bustle.

Plants have a similar effect on our homes. What other decorations can you see grow and evolve over time? One day you might see a new sprout or even flowers starting to blossom and bloom, marking the beginning of a season. And if you get plants through clippings or when they're very young, you can often get them cheaper than any painting or knick-knack.

In fact, people like looking at plants so much that we have created an entire industry dedicated to the manufacturing of fake plants. But why get a fake plant when you can have the real thing? Real plants look better: they are living, growing things that we can connect with and take care of while we enjoy their beauty.

Plants quiet our busy minds

In today's era of social media, smartphones, highways and shopping malls, plants keep us rooted to the natural world. How many times through the day are your thoughts disrupted by notifications? It's easy to get wrapped up in the fast-paced world of news, business and entertainment. If we're not careful, we can sit in front of a screen and 'poof', the whole day has passed. Our eyes are strained, our bodies are confined to our chairs and we haven't given our minds a break.

Wellness experts support growing plants as a way of staying centred. Best-selling author and fitness guru Deanne Panday once told me on a call, 'Gardening, much like grooming, clean eating and good fitness, is a welcome addition to our daily health routine. It's a simple tool anyone can use to destress.'

She's right. Gardening puts me in a state of meditation. When I garden, I'm in the moment, completely immersed in my plants. All my doubts, worries and concerns melt away. I'm not multitasking, checking my phone or thinking about the topic of my next meeting. I'm just thinking about plants.

For however long I am gardening, whether it is fifteen minutes, half an hour or the entire morning, for that period of time, I am engrossed. When I start the day focused on plants, I feel collected and present throughout the rest of the day. Even when I get on social media to post a video to Lazy Gardener, I find that I am less distracted by other apps and images on my feed. The practice of gardening extends beyond the growth of our plants. It develops us as people, too.

Plants teach us patience

Patience is not always a prized possession in today's world. Businesses have cleverly designed their stores, technology and supply chains to give us what we want, when we want it. Less than twenty years ago, shipping took weeks if not months. Now, we can often get almost anything delivered to our homes in days or even hours. In 1990, when my father was helping set up a university in Bhutan, he and I wrote letters to one another. It took weeks for me to get a reply. Now, we have instant messaging so we can reach almost anyone immediately, no matter where they are in the world. This instant gratification is convenient in the moment, but it has trained us to become easily frustrated when we don't see results right away.

Gardening is a way to remind ourselves that it takes time to cultivate and grow beauty in our lives. Long-term happiness requires patience. Plants don't grow at the click of a button; they demand consistent care. When you water a plant or move it into a different light, the plant won't react immediately. It takes a few days—if not weeks—to see new growth.

These small changes are rewarding because of the time we spent waiting in anticipation. The good thing about plants is that they are fairly forgiving. One day of neglect isn't going to kill your plant, just like one day of attention isn't going to turn it into a ten-foot tree. It's not about what you do in any one day, but about giving your plant consistent care over time, practising patience and observing it grow.

Patience is also the cornerstone of love. The dedication we have to our plants is the same kind of dedication it takes to form healthy, long-lasting relationships with a good friend, a lover or a family member. Just as it is important to understand our loved ones' needs and desires, it is also important to understand what our plants enjoy and how we can help them grow. We know that our plants can live on their own and be happy without being constantly watched, but we have to commit to keeping our plants in mind for years and years if we want them to continue growing under our care.

The value of patience is universal. I noticed that when Mili was born, Keerti had to not only learn to be a patient mother but also had to teach Mili how to be a patient child. When Keerti helped Mili sow some rajma seeds, Mili began to understand the beauty of patience. Initially, she checked them at every meal time to see if they had sprouted, but soon she learnt that what she had sown would take time to grow, which made it all more exciting and satisfying when they finally sprouted. Most children are eager to get their hands dirty and begin planting seeds, but then they have to wait, which is when they learn the real lesson. When we sow the seeds of patience, we are growing the fruit of a more harmonious world.

(To learn how to grow rajma seeds and other plant activities for parents and children, read the chapter on Building a Community, starting on p. 204).

Plants make us feel at home

One of the first things I do whenever I move to a new space is bring in some plants. They remind me of the simple, wonderful moments of my life: spending time outdoors with my family; climbing trees on the playground; and making new friends with other plant lovers. Whenever I move to a new home, hostel or office desk, I always bring a money plant; even a single cutting in a glass of water makes me think of home.

There are many different types of plants that are called 'money plants', depending on where you are in the world, but in India, the plant that is referred to as the 'money plant' is the golden pothos (*Epipremnum aureum*, also called ' devil's ivy'). Indians have a strong emotional connection with the golden pothos because they are found throughout the country, and they are one of the easiest plants to propagate and grow indoors. Money plants are so pervasive in gardens and parks that I often like to joke that you might as well 'steal' a cutting to propagate. Some people even say that money plants are only lucky if you pick them from the wild or receive them as a gift. I can move anywhere in the world and no matter how far I am from New Delhi, keeping a money plant in my space makes me feel more at home.

You might have an attachment to your own favourite plant. I know many people who fill their living rooms with monstera and snake plants, or cover their balconies with tulsi (holy basil), aloe vera, hibiscus and marigold. A lot of people, like my mamiji, put flowers around their homes because the aroma is calming and instantly reminds them of their youth.

Plants make our guests feel at home when they visit us, too. Like an interesting table or piece of art, plants are a great topic of conversation. Whenever people visit, they often look at all my plants and ask me, 'What's this one?' Or, if they know the plant, they might have a story or a memory to share. I've learnt a lot about my guests just by talking about plants. One of my favourite places to meet new people isn't the coffee shop but the local nursery.

I love to see how people use plants to make their homes feel welcoming and alive. If you have plants in your home, I would love to see them! Share a picture of your plants at home on Instagram, Facebook or Twitter, tag @lazygardener.in and use the hashtag #HowtoRaiseaPlantBaby

Plants bring people together

Plants are a gift to us from nature, and a gift that we can give to each other. Throughout history, plants have played a central role in building culture and society. Early in human history, people worked together to forage for fruit, nuts and berries. Later, we formed communities around the growing of crops. Today, friends and family come together in parks and gardens to enjoy a picnic or a pleasant afternoon. I have many great memories of picnics with classmates, friends and family members at Lodhi Gardens in Delhi.

When we garden together, it strengthens our relationships; we create little inside jokes and share the rewards of small wins such as seeing a seed germinate, a leaf unfurl or a flower bloom. And if you're growing food in a neighbourhood garden, there's the added enjoyment of eating together as a community. The shared experience of nurturing something from seed to plate can bring together even people with very different ideas.

Especially now that many green spaces are in danger of being converted into another road or building, people can unite over plants. I strengthened my bonds with my neighbours when we came together to save Shiva Vatika Park. It was a big win that we can all look back on collectively with feelings of joy. We continued to improve the park, adding a compost area and a champa grove. Every spring, the park is full of flowering petunias, pansies, salvias, chrysanthemums and more. Today, Shiva Vatika Park is very popular, bringing more people together than ever.

I'm a huge advocate of schools, teachers, parents and communities teaching younger generations the importance of plants so that plants can once again become a part of our daily lives. Even when we simply trade plant cuttings, we're sharing a memory with our friends, family members or loved ones. They can look at a plant and say, 'Remember when you gave this to me? It was just a cutting!'

We all have something to gain from more plants in our lives, so in a way, they are a common denominator—something that we can celebrate, care about and find joy in.

Plants make life possible

Often it may seem as if we're the ones taking care of plants, but they take care of us, too. Plants produce two things we rely on to survive: oxygen and glucose. We need oxygen to breathe, and we need glucose to create energy within our bodies.

When we see images of earth from space, the first thing we notice is the blue of the water and the green of the plants. Plants are the earth's lungs, functioning as natural air purifiers by absorbing carbon dioxide and other toxins and releasing oxygen. When we breathe, plants breathe with us. So far, we have not found another planet flourishing with plants, so it is even more important to take care of the plants we have here on earth. They may be the only plants in the entire universe.

New Delhi, where I live, is one of the smoggiest cities in the world. Vehicle exhaust emissions, factories, crop burning and construction have clouded the air. Dense plumes of pollution stay suspended in the city year-round, making it difficult to see more than ten metres in front of our faces. This air pollution causes headaches, skin irritation and eye irritation, among other ailments. According to the World Health Organization, India has the world's highest death rate from chronic respiratory diseases and asthma.*

Some people keep indoor plants to clean up the air around them. Unfortunately, a few plants won't make a big difference in the air we breathe every day. The most impactful way for us to decrease air pollution is to address the things that cause the air to become polluted in the first place.

However, we should also conserve as many trees and plants as possible while planting new trees for the future. The essential nature of trees can be easy to forget if we don't interact with plants in our day-to-day lives. When your internet goes down, you might feel like you have lost something essential, especially

---

* https://www.who.int/news-room/fact-sheets/detail/asthma

if you use the internet for your job. But do you feel the same way when you walk or drive past a tree that has been cut down?

The plants that absorb the most carbon dioxide and release the most oxygen are often large trees that take hundreds of years to grow. In one season, a large, leafy tree typically produces enough oxygen for a small group of people to breathe for an entire year, while absorbing tons of carbon dioxide in the process. Taking care of plants indoors is a good reminder of how much time it takes to grow a plant, helping incentivize us to preserve the powerhouse plants outside in our community.

There are times when I feel that, as humans, we get a little ahead of ourselves. We have made enormous strides when it comes to creating homes, vehicles and entire infrastructures that make it easier to survive as a society. Many of these technologies have given us the opportunity to grow by connecting people to jobs, improving mobility and expanding housing and other vital community spaces.

But as we have grown, we have also jeopardized the plants and natural balance that are fundamental to our existence. Urbanization across India, much like the changes I have seen in my parents' neighbourhood in New Delhi, has greatly impacted the amount of space we have to live in and the amount of green spaces in our country. Meanwhile, the air above our homes continues to become more polluted as we accelerate global climate change.

Humans can survive without the internet. It would be much harder to survive without trees. We need to find more sustainable ways to create energy, build homes and manage our use of the earth's resources. But part of creating a future that can sustain humans indefinitely relies on us understanding, appreciating and acknowledging the vital role of plants.

2

Common Plant Myths and Questions

Plants are the backbone of the natural world. Life on earth depends on plants, yet many people find them mysterious. And with anything that we have half-knowledge about, we tend to string together our own myths and theories. I've met people who doubt their ability to keep plants alive because they believe they don't have a green thumb. I've met others who are scared to keep plants at home because they think that plants will harm them in their sleep. On the other hand, I've met plant lovers who exaggerate the positive effects plants can have, believing that a single plant can solve indoor air pollution.

Every myth is rooted in some level of truth. Plant myths are no different. We all learn about plants when we are children— that they release oxygen through photosynthesis and consume it through respiration. Our imagination can take these facts and quickly lead us to false conclusions such as how a single plant can clean the air in our homes, or that plants will steal oxygen from us.

Many myths stem from our worries or our desires. We need to be careful to temper our hopes and fears because we could end up listening to advice that could harm our plants. For instance, a plant parent may become so worried that their plant isn't getting enough water that they overwater and kill their plant.

Of course, the great and powerful internet has a lot of good information for plant parents, but it is also where loads of misinformation is propagated. First, we must be careful what we search for. It's better to search for information from a plant's perspective than from your own. Open-ended questions like 'What is the ideal climate for monstera?' will usually provide you with better guidance. But when you search for questions to which the answers can only be 'yes' or 'no', such as 'Will monstera survive in my living room?' you will often get information that is incomplete or just plain wrong. Sure, you can grow monstera in most living rooms, but is your home in the right climate? Where in your living room should you keep it? You're more likely to find the answers you need when you ask open-ended questions.

Even when you find an answer online, it is important to consider the bias of the person providing that information. Are they from the same part of the world as you are? If not, their plant advice will be different from the advice you need to grow plants in your climate. In my videos, I often discourage people from buying and growing succulents because they do not grow well in Delhi and most parts of India. But if you're in the Himalayas, succulents are easy plants to grow.

If we are to become great caretakers of our plants, it is important to have a solid grasp on our imagined hopes and fears so that we can focus on what plants actually provide, and what we can do to provide for our plants.

To set the record straight, I want to take some time to examine a few common myths about plants, discuss how these myths came to be and explore the truth behind them.

Myth: I do not have a green thumb. My plants always die.

Is there such a thing as a green thumb? If I kill a plant, does this mean that I was not born to be a gardener?

As much as we like to believe that we are born with certain skills, most of the things we are good at in life take time and practise. And caring for plants is no different. Yes, you may have certain talents and skills that may prepare you for being a plant parent, but the truth is that anyone can learn to care for plants and help them grow.

Here's where the shocking truth comes out: yes, I have killed a plant before. In fact, I have killed many plants by accident. Now, before you close this book and say, 'Why should I trust Vinayak the plant murderer!' it is important to realize that I wouldn't know all the things I am sharing with you if I had not gone through the trial and error that has led to some of my plants withering away. It is also important to know that even if you follow all my advice, you are probably still going to have a plant die on you. This does not make you a bad plant parent. Instead, it is an opportunity for you to learn, grow and try again.

Sometimes it will be obvious why your plant died. If it looks burnt to a crisp, it was probably too close to direct light or a heat source in your home. If it starts to wilt, you probably didn't water it enough or are watering it too much. Other times, the reason why your plant dies will not be so obvious. Sometimes plants have something going on beneath the soil that we do not know about.

I am here to tell you that you *can* be a plant parent, and that plants dying is part of the process. The fact that you are reading this book means that you are investing your time, and it is likely to pay off. Our goal is to keep plants alive and help them grow, but it is important not to give up. Persevere, keep trying and pay attention to your plants, and you too will be an amazing plant parent.

Myth: People who travel can't keep plants.

If I travel, how will my plants stay alive? Who will water them? What if I come back to a plant graveyard?

Many people who travel a lot for work or as a family believe that they cannot own a plant. If they are gone from their home for weeks at a time, will the plants die? Maybe some plants will, such as fittonia and fiddle leaf, which need a lot of attention. But there are also many plants that are relatively self-reliant, such as succulents and snake plants.

When New Delhi was locked down at the start of the COVID-19 pandemic in 2020, I had some ZZ plants, philodendrons and snake plants trapped in my office. I watered them before I left, and these plants are good at storing water, but I was still worried about them. Six weeks later, when I was finally able to check on my plants, I found that they were still alive and healthy.

Plants are tougher than you might think; they can endure drought, infestation and all sorts of hazards in the wild. Chances are your plants can survive a few weeks alone in your home. The ZZ plant, the snake plant, certain types of philodendron, cacti, aloe, jade, the spider plant and the rubber plant are all drought-friendly varieties that can survive for weeks without being watered, especially if the plant is more mature.

It is just a matter of picking the right plant for your lifestyle. If you know that you travel a lot, try to own plants that do not need as much water. You may not want to buy a baby plant and leave it in your home the day before you leave town, but a sturdy snake plant that has settled in will be fine without you for a while.

Myth: Plants bring bugs inside.

You have probably seen bugs crawling around in the dirt before. So, if you bring a plant inside, are you inviting bugs inside, too?

Probably not. It is true that bugs such as caterpillars and ants live in the soil and snack on plants. But the soil you keep in a pot is only a small part of an insect's ecosystem. Insects are a bigger problem in outdoor gardens where they are free to roam and snack on many plants. When we put plants in a pot, it is easier to prevent bugs from making the soil their home.

Take it from me: I do not like bugs at all. In fact, I am a bit afraid of them. Once in a while, I may find a spider mite or a snail trying to sneak into my house on a potted pothos that I am bringing inside. If I see a snail on a leaf, I simply prune the leaf with the snail on it, take it outside, and help it transfer to another branch or leaf so it can continue on its way. For the most part, I never cross paths with insects, even if they are living inside the pot. Most insects stay in their own homes, deep in the soil. They have no interest in invading where you live.

Some people ask if plants attract mosquitoes. Mosquitos are not attracted to your plants. They are attracted to standing water; they are looking for a dark, moist area to breed. But if you water your plants properly, there should not be any standing water for the mosquitoes to lay their eggs in, which will prevent them from flying around your plants.

It is more likely that pests are coming inside for warmth or food, not to seek out your plant. The best thing you can do to prevent bugs from coming inside is to find any small cracks or holes that they can crawl through and seal them. Bugs might also come through your windows and doors if you leave them open but using a mesh screen can prevent most bugs from finding their way inside. Sealing any access points will make a far greater difference than getting rid of your plants.

I always recommend that when someone buys a new plant, they keep it outside on their balcony or porch for a week or two to observe and ensure that no insects are living on the leaves or in the soil. Once it is confirmed that no insects are living in the pot, it is safe to bring inside. If you do notice that insects have taken to a plant inside your home, move it outside, put on glove and carefully attempt to repot the plant while removing any and all insects you find in the soil. Don't blame the plant. Just care for it and remove the buggies.

Myth: Plants will kill me in my sleep.

Have you ever heard the story of someone dying in their sleep because a plant stole their oxygen? Or the myth about someone falling asleep under a banyan tree that killed them in their sleep?

This has never happened. While getting killed by a tree or a plant is a very frightening thought, I assure you that plants will not suffocate you in your sleep. If they did, all the animals in the rainforest would be dead.

Compared to trees in the rainforest, the plants we keep in our homes are tiny. They will never affect your breathing. Meanwhile, the people you share your home with release far more CO_2 into the air than any plant in your home. Do you freak out when you have guests over for dinner? If a person can visit for the evening without any trouble, your monstera should not be an issue either.

Myth: Plants improve indoor air quality.

Have you heard that keeping plants inside will clean the air in your home? Just as some people imagine that plants 'steal oxygen', others exaggerate the impact plants have on indoor air quality. The truth is that it takes a lot of plants to make any perceivable impact. There have been studies (most famously a NASA study*) that show that plants can absorb volatile organic compounds such as formaldehyde and nitrous oxide. However, they do so on such a small scale that it will not make a difference in your home. Moreover, the studies show that it is the roots of the plants that help absorb the harmful organic compounds efficiently rather than the leaves themselves.

Plants do produce oxygen, but most of us don't have the time, space or resources for the amount of plants we would need to improve air quality. You would need about thirty plants per square metre to make an impact. At that point, you might have fresh air to breathe, but you'll have nowhere to sleep or walk without stepping on your plants. I know I just said plants don't bring insects inside, but with that many plants, bugs might confuse your indoor space with an outdoor garden and make themselves at home.

If you are concerned about indoor air quality, plants are probably not the answer. While plants do not *hurt* indoor air quality, they also do not *improve* the air quality in any noticeable way. Instead, plants help us breathe easy because they decrease our stress levels and make us more comfortable in our own homes.

---

* https://ntrs.nasa.gov/api/citations/19930073077/downloads/19930073077.pdf

Myth: Plants need to be outside.

Can plants truly be happy inside our homes?

Plants naturally come from outside, so it is fair to think that they belong outside. But plants do not think in terms of 'indoor' and 'outdoor'. For many plants, as long as they have their roots planted in soil, some light hitting their leaves and water to drink up through their roots, they are happy. And we can create these conditions in our homes!

The light in your home and the light outside are almost the same. When you walk around outside, you will notice that there are areas of bright light and varying levels of shade. Different plants naturally grow in these different light conditions, and they can all be replicated in our homes by placing our plants closer to or further from our windows. Even some lights we have inside, such as light bulbs, are good for plants. Although standard indoor lights are not as useful as natural sunlight or grow lamps, these lights are still useful enough to grow a healthy plant.

The truth is that there are no 'indoor plants'. There are plants that like bright light and there are plants that prefer less light. When we bring plants into our homes, it is important to consider where that plant grows in nature so that we can find the best place for that plant in our home.

Myth: Water is always the answer.

How often do plants need water? Some people say, 'Every day! Plants love water!'

Although all plants need water to make food, the most common reason people accidentally kill their plants is that they give them *too much* water. As a kid, even though I grew up around gardening, I was taught to give plants water whenever there was a problem. But there are many other factors to consider, such as the light, the soil, the pot, the humidity, insects and diseases that can harm plants. Now, when I see a sick plant, I consider all the factors instead of going straight to 'it needs water'. I learnt the hard way that water is not always the answer.

A good rule of thumb is that it is better for your plants to be thirsty than to be drowning in water. Plants can recover more easily from lack of water than they can from something like root rot.

Myth: Expensive means better.

The most expensive plants are the best, right? Otherwise why would they cost all that money?

Typically, higher-quality goods are more expensive. But plants are not manufactured like furniture, technology or clothing. It is easy to say that one chair is better than another chair based on how comfortable it is, what material it is made from or how much support it provides. But plants are not standardized; they are all unique.

There are three factors that nurseries and plant sellers use to determine the price of their plants:

1.   How mature the plant is
2.   How far it has travelled to reach the nursery
3.   How rare the plant is

It takes time for plants to grow, and in a consumer culture, time is money. So, if you are taking a shortcut and buying a tree that already has fruit, you can expect to pay more.

Now, does bigger mean better? Maybe to some people who want a large, lush plant for decoration. But I believe that it is better to start with a small plant. You will save money, and the best part is that you will learn more about what that plant likes and does not like. You will be more prepared to take care of it when it is a mature plant. Many new gardeners who start with a mature plant have a difficult time keeping it alive because they did not help it get to that size, so they do not know what makes that plant happy. Also, it is a rewarding feeling to watch a plant grow from a baby plant into something tall and sturdy.

Whenever you buy a plant that is not local or does not naturally grow nearby, it costs more because of transportation. You're paying extra not only for the cost of fuel, but also for the plants that died during the trip. You will have a better chance of success if you purchase a plant that is native to your area, so you may want to ask yourself if it is worth the extra cost for a non-native plant that is hard to take care of.

Rare plants like black anthurium or variegated monstera can cost an absurd amount just for a cutting. Some of these high prices are driven by online trends. A popular gardener may post a rare plant on Instagram or YouTube, and suddenly half of their followers want to buy this plant, and plant sellers may raise the price due to the demand. But is it worth buying that rare plant?

The heart wants what the heart wants, but you do not need to buy a Picasso to appreciate art. There are thousands of different species of plants that you can buy, and you can never buy them all. The important thing is to pick the plant that is right for you.

If you are new to gardening, start small. You can find a nice plant that will make you happy and teach you everything you need to know without spending a lot of money. You might even be able to get a nice plant for free. We will talk about some of my favourite plants later in the book so you can figure out what plant to start with.

3

The Types of Plants We Grow at Home

There are more than 3,00,000 different plant species, but the good news is that you don't need to know about every plant in the world to be a good plant parent. Even avid gardeners like myself don't know every species of plant or all their scientific names and classifications.

But I do know enough about plants to look at a new plant and determine what it might need to survive in my home. It helps to be able to notice if a plant can store water and think to ourselves, 'That plant can go a while without watering' or see that a plant has nodes along its stem and think, 'Maybe I should get a moss stick for this plant to nurture the roots along the stem.'

I generally group houseplants into four categories:

- Storage houses: plants that store water
- Wanderers: plants with aerial roots
- Blooming wonders: plants that grow flowers, even indoors
- Stiff and sterns: trees and plants with woody stems

Examples of Storage houses: Plants that store water

These four categories are by no means scientific or complete, but they give us good guidance as plant parents. I've given each category a simple name that is easy to remember. There are a few outlier plants such as orchids and carnivorous plants that defy these characteristics. There are also plants that combine characteristics from two or more of these types: bougainvillea grows flowers like a blooming wonder but has a stiff branching structure similar to a stiff and stern. But these four categories cover about 90 per cent of houseplants.

My intent is to teach you how to look at plants and have a basic understanding of what your plants need, what they like and how to respond to different scenarios.

When you know a plant's category, you'll have a better understanding of:

- How it likes to be watered
- How much water it needs
- How to propagate your plant
- What kind of growth to expect from your plant

- What type of environment your plant likes
- Where to place your plant in your home
- How easy or difficult your plant is to care for

Storage houses: Plants that store water

All plants take in water and use it to make food, which we will cover when we talk about photosynthesis. But some plants store water in their leaves, roots or stems.

Let's look at a snake plant. Snake plants have long, thick, waxy leaves. If we cut the leaf of a snake plant open, we can see that it is fleshy inside; it's kind of goopy and green and holds a thick liquid. You'll notice the same thing with jade plants and succulents—thick, fleshy leaves. All these plants store water in their leaves, which is why they are thick. In fact, the word 'succulent' comes from the Latin word *succus*, which means 'juicy' or ' to hold water'.

Other plants, such as cacti, have thick, stalky stems that can store water. There are also plants such as ZZ plants and rain lilies that hide their water storage tanks underground in the form of bulb roots!

Plants that have a spongy, water-storing part can be categorized as storage houses. You may be more familiar with storage houses than you think because we eat many parts of plants that store water underground, including onions and potatoes! I have some exercises later in the book where you can learn how bulb plants store water and grow new plants.

So why do plants such as jade, snake plants and succulents hold water? Because they come from deserts and other dry areas that experience long droughts. When we think of desert animals we often think of camels, who also store water in the large humps on their backs. It's fascinating that both plants and animals have adapted to dry areas by storing water!

Now, if we know that these plants store water, how does this change the way we take care of them? It's simple: we water them less. Because storage houses have adapted to drier climates, you must be extra careful to give them plenty of light and not overwater them.

When grown in low-light conditions, like inside your home or on a balcony, storage houses do not need as much water as other types of plants because they are good at retaining water. Storage houses that store water in their leaves, such as succulents and snake plants, can survive high heat, a lot of sunlight and long periods of drought. But if these plants get *too much* water, they are likely to develop root rot.

Storage houses are typically easy to propagate, and many of them actually self-propagate. Some storage houses like snake plants can even be propagated using only the leaf, which we will touch upon in the propagation section of this book.

Wanderers: Plants that grow aerial roots

I mentioned that, for most plants, we only want to water the soil because that's where the roots are. But there are a few plants that grow roots along the stem. These plants like to grow in many directions and seek out water *above* the soil. Because these plants like to wander around with their stems, I like to call them wanderers.

Let's look at money plants (pothos). Money plants grow long stems that are sectioned by nodes. Each of these nodes is an area where roots can sprout and grow. In nature, wanderers grow under the shade of many other plants and have to compete for water and sunlight. Their goal then becomes to grow upwards, higher and higher, eventually peaking above the canopy. When they grow, the roots along the vine grab on to trees and taller plants to get water as their stems move up the tree. We call these roots along the vines 'aerial roots'.

Pothos, syngonium, monstera and Wandering Jew are all examples of wanderers that have nodes from which aerial roots can sprout.

Since nodes and aerial roots indicate that the plant grows naturally under and around trees, it means that any wanderer enjoys low-to-medium light. But because we often forget to water the aerial roots, many wanderers that we see indoors never develop roots along their stems or grow as big as they do in the jungle.

With wanderers, it is important to water not only the soil but also the nodes so that the leaves further away from the soil can grow big and healthy and capture more light.

Think about the plant's stem like a giant straw. The longer the straw, the more suction (energy) it takes to pull the water all the way through. Luckily, the aerial roots make the distance shorter, but only if we give them the opportunity to take in water.

If you have a wanderer, I recommend buying a spray bottle and spraying the nodes with a mist of water every couple of weeks—more when the season is hot and sunny, and less when it is not sunny. Putting moisture near the nodes along the stems will encourage them to sprout roots because the plant will think, 'There is water here. Let me extend my roots to investigate.' Once you notice roots along the stems of your wanderer, you can then guide it, much like the plant would naturally guide itself up a tree if it were in the jungle.

There are two ways I like to guide my wanderers: one is with a string and damp cloth, and the other is with a moss stick.

Guiding wanderers with string and paper towels

I like to give my money plants some string to help them wander. Here, I used a length of twine that my money plant stem can wrap around and grow along. You'll notice that I have placed a damp paper towel wherever there are aerial roots. I use paper towels because

A money plant vine growing along a string

they absorb and hold water, much like dirt, but you can use any lightweight, absorbent material.

Whenever I notice the towel is dry, I pour more water onto it. I have found that you can keep using the same paper towels for a while because they can dry out and keep absorbing water. I've used some paper towels for over a year without any problems. You'll notice that the leaves at the end are just as big as the leaves near the bottom, thanks to the paper towels.

I like to get creative and guide my money plant along my ceiling and over archways. If I really want to make my money plant feel like it is in the jungle, I can even guide it to a tree on my balcony and let the end of it grow up towards the sun.

Guiding wanderers with a moss stick

You may not like how the napkins look along your plant. Another option is to buy a moss stick from your nursery and plant it towards the edge of your pot. As your wanderer grows, you can guide it up the moss stick, where the roots along the stem can grab on and soak up moisture. If you use a moss stick, it is important to pour water above and down into the moss stick so that it can provide moisture to the aerial roots. Water your moss stick just as you would water the soil: wait until it is completely dry, and water it thoroughly.

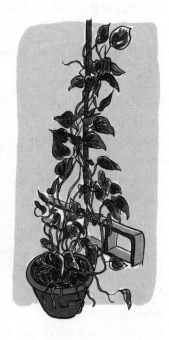

An aerial root plant growing up a moss stick

Because wanderers are often segmented into nodes, they are easy to propagate with a cutting of the stem that includes at least one node. We will discuss how to propagate wanderers in the propagation chapter of this book.

Blooming wonders: Flowering plants for your home

I like to categorize blooming wonders as plants that flower profusely and are included in home garden specifically for their flowers. Blooming wonders are often regarded for their colours and beauty and are popular with interior decorators who like to use flowering plants to accent homes.

Some wanderers, such as money plants and monsteras, can blossom if they get enough light, but they rarely blossom indoors or in low-light conditions.

But why do these blooming wonders grow flowers? The answer is simple: plants grow flowers to reproduce. This gets us to the age-old question: where do plant babies come from?

Many plants can be propagated, but flowering plants have a different method for making new plants. Inside every flower is pollen and a pollen tube. Wind and insects such as bees and butterflies can move the pollen from flower to flower, encouraging the plant to produce seeds. The seeds can then be used to grow more blooming wonders.

Blooming wonders: Flowering plants for your home

Insects are more effective at moving pollen from flower to flower than wind, so many flowering plants have adapted to produce bright colours, lovely smells and delicious nectar that attract fuzzy insects such as honeybees.

There are two general kinds of blooming wonders: seasonal plants and perennials.

Seasonal blooming wonders will survive for only one season, and they typically grow only in bright sunlight. You will need to replant seeds for these types of blooming wonders if you want to keep them in your home or garden. Seasonal blooming wonders are ideal for the balcony or veranda and include plants such as petunias and pansies.

Perennial blooming wonders last for more than one season and continue to blossom throughout the year. Perennials include plants such as the peace lily and anthurium.

The main characteristic of blooming wonders is that they grow flowers. But even when they're not blooming, you will notice that almost all blooming wonders have green, soft stems.

Because these plants grow flowers, they require plenty of phosphorus, light and water. So, if you are growing any blooming wonders, make sure to give them fertilizer with plenty of phosphorus. These plants can be a little tricky to grow, but if you give them love and attention, they will reward you with their lovely look and smell.

All blooming wonders require bright light for flowering with an exception of anthurium and peace lily. Even anthurium and peace lily would flower better if given brighter light.

Stiff and sterns: Trees and plants with woody stems

Stiff and sterns are essentially small trees or shrubs such as fiddle leaf figs, lemon trees or bougainvillea.

Stiff and sterns almost always have a rough exterior, which is what makes them so stiff. Because these plants often grow to be larger than most plants and can often bear fruit, they need the added support of their rough exterior to hold themselves up.

In nature, stiff and sterns grow in forests or grasslands where they need to defend themselves from animals that eat their

Stiff and sterns: Trees and plants with woody stems

fruit or haphazardly trample around them. You'll also notice that many of these plants develop defence mechanisms such as bristles and thorns on their stems and branches.

Stiff and sterns require plenty of patience to grow because they take a lot of time to get to the size where they bear fruit or grow the large, lovely leaves they're known for. When you grow these plants at home, they can be tricky because they need a lot of light, but they are susceptible to being burnt by heat.

In nature, stiff and sterns are used to growing around other tall plants. For example, a sapling lemon tree in a grove might receive shade from another lemon tree that keeps it cool, but still receive plenty of light through the foliage. A lot of people have trouble growing fiddle leaf figs because they either grow them inside where they don't get enough light, or they grow them outside on a balcony where it is too hot. In nature, they might have just the right balance, but in our homes, it can be harder to create the right conditions for these stiff and sterns.

Many stiff and sterns can be propagated through air layering, which we will cover in the propagation chapter of this book.

Water, light and soil requirements for types of plants

Plant type	Water	Light	Soil
Storage houses	Less frequent watering. Dry spells between watering is preferred	Bright light or direct sun preferred for most (Snake plant and ZZ can tolerate low light)	High drainage soil like sand. Avoid coco peat
Wanderers	Enjoy humidity and frequent watering	Tolerate low light. Do better in bright light. Don't like direct sun	Medium drainage loamy soil. Mix of coarse material in soil is helpful
Blooming wonders	Frequent watering, especially when flowering	Bright light and direct sun required	Medium drainage loamy soil
Stiff and sterns	Frequent watering required. Let the soil dry in-between watering	Bright light or direct sun preferred for most	Medium drainage soil. Soil is required to provide ample support to the plant

4

The Journey of Houseplants: How Plants Get to You

Plants, like people, have diverse stories about how they got from where they started to where they are today. Some come from other countries. Other plants are born here, either in nurseries or from seeds and cuttings exchanged among plant parents. Many types of plants that are grown in India originated somewhere else but have been here for generations because they have acclimated to our environment.

One major change I have noticed over the past decade is that most local nurseries in India no longer grow their own plants because it is not commercially viable. Most of the plant supply is controlled by plantations and wholesale nurseries in Pune, Kolkata and Kadiyam. Plantations specialize in creating new plants from cuttings and seeds, while wholesale nurseries specialize in importing plants and distributing them to smaller nurseries across the country.

A few years ago, I asked a local nursery in Delhi why they were not growing their own roses anymore, and they said, 'By the time we can start trimming our roses, Pune has already flooded the market with blooming roses. There's no way to compete.'

Since there are only a few hubs that specialize in importing and growing plants, any plant that you find in a nursery has travelled a long way to get there. We want to be careful not to purchase a plant that has just arrived at the nursery. It is better to give plants time to rest and recover after their long journey. Once they have had time to acclimate to their new home in Delhi or Bengaluru or Jaipur or wherever you are, then they will have the strength and energy to be ready for their final move to your home.

Remember that every day, thousands of plants are moved across the country, and they go through a lot of stress on their journey. They are constantly being packed, unpacked and lifted in and out of cargo trucks. Some plants are even imported by ship or by plane, enduring all kinds of rough water and turbulence before they arrive. Good thing plants do not have stomachs and are already green, else they would show signs of motion sickness after such a long journey!

What you may notice are signs of physical damage like torn leaves on plants that have taken a long trip to get to your local nursery. As a plant lover, you may be thinking, 'Why are nurseries and malis so rough on the plants?' Fortunately, plants are strong. In nature, they survive being nibbled on by insects and herbivores, and trampled on by large animals. I try not to be too concerned about physical damage, and instead focus on whether or not there are signs that the plant has acclimated to the nursery. What I am really looking for is new growth: a fresh stem or leaf poking out from the soil. I will talk more about what to look for when shopping for a plant in the next chapter.

Exotic plants versus native or naturalized plants

When I was younger, there was less of a frenzy over exotic plants. Before the internet, plant envy was limited to neighbours; there were no influencers on social media showing off their fancy plants to people around the world. People were still discovering plants in their nearby parks, gardens and local nurseries. We would visit a friend or neighbour, see a new plant and ask, 'What plant is that?' while thinking 'I want one, too!'

Today, people discover plants online, which leads to new gardeners becoming more excited about exotic plants than the plants around their neighbourhood. But buying an exotic plant just to show off on social media is often less fulfilling than starting with a local plant that nurtures your growth as a gardener.

I always advise new gardeners to start with a native or naturalized plant instead of an exotic one for three reasons:

1. They are far easier to take care of
2. They are much cheaper
3. They connect us to our community

Because native plants have grown in our parks and gardens for generations, they are designed for our lifestyle. With these plants, we do not have to obsess about putting them in the wrong light or giving them too much or too little water. Instead, we can take our time to learn and celebrate new growth milestones without getting overwhelmed by watching an expensive plant die before our eyes.

Sometimes, you can get native plants for free because they are so easy to find and propagate. Exotic plants, on the other hand, are expensive because they have to be shipped from another country.

Native plants also have deep roots in our culture. Taking care of native plants is a great way to celebrate who we are and where we come from. I love when someone visits their hometown, notices a plant that they remember from their childhood, and it stirs up memories of their family and what life was like when they were growing up. It is like the difference between making parathas with your grandmother and eating alone at a five -star Italian restaurant. The meal at the restaurant may be fancy and exotic, but nothing can replace grandma's cooking, or the experience of spending time with the people you love.

I know common plants may not be as immediately exciting as that pink princess or variegated monstera you saw online. Maybe you already have an image in your head of a large, lush garden with plants from countries around the world. And I am not going to lie and say that I have not spent more money than I should have on a fancy plant. There is an appeal to an expensive 'YouTube' plant, but if you are going to make that investment, make sure that you are confident in your plant knowledge and instincts. It is better to start small and cheap so you do not feel you wasted your money if you accidentally kill your plant.

The good news is that you have plenty of options to choose from. A wide variety of storage houses, wanderers, blooming wonders, and stiff and sterns are native to India or have been naturalized. Money plants, plumeria, madhumalti creeper or Song of India are all a great place to start because you can take a few cuttings from a public park or a friend's house, propagate a bunch, and if some die, it is no big deal. After you get used to taking care of an easy, abundant plant, you can upgrade to something a little more fragile, like a snake plant, and then work your way up until you feel comfortable spending money on a plant that is going to be more of a challenge. You can always buy the more exotic plants later.

Sometimes, the line between 'native' and 'exotic' is not so clear. A lot of plants that start out as exotic become popular and then become acclimatized over time. There was a time when even the Song of India was an exotic plant since it first came from the island of Madagascar. Recently I've noticed that there are some plants that have quickly become well-suited to India's climate after exploding in popularity online, like the ZZ plant.

How long does it take plants to get used to a new area?

Although new to India, the ZZ plant is common here today, thanks to YouTube. I remember the first time I saw it in a nursery around 2015. I recognized the plant but could not remember the name. So I looked it up on my phone, and I found a bunch of YouTube videos about ZZ plants. The person at the nursery peeked at my phone and said, 'Yes, this is the YouTube plant.'

Before then, I had never seen a ZZ plant in person. Many older generations do not even recognize it. The ZZ plant is originally from the grasslands of Africa, which have a similar climate and latitude to India. Now, when I go to the nursery, it is easy to find a healthy ZZ plant.

But not all plants become well-suited to a new area, especially if they come from a totally different climate. Succulents have also become popular in India, but they are not easy to grow unless you are in the Himalayas. Succulents grow in desert areas, so they are used to being dry and dealing with shifts from hot to cold. In our home, we typically keep the temperature around twenty-two degree Celsius, which is better for tropical plants that enjoy being warm all year long. Even though they are interesting plants, I advise most beginner gardeners to avoid buying succulents unless they are okay with the fact that these plants will likely die within a season.

Bougainvillea is another plant that is not native to India but has popped up all over the country since reaching our shores. It originally comes from Brazil and other parts of South America. Bougainvillea was first introduced to India around 1860, and much like the ZZ plant, it does well in our warm, subtropical climate. In fact, without any care or attention at all, bougainvillea plants reward us with their colourful blooms. Bougainvillea is part blooming wonder and part stiff and stern, so it is both hearty and beautiful, which is why city planners and developers grow them on road dividers. If you have ever driven a long distance in India, you will probably recognize their beautiful pink, white and yellow flowers as soon as you see them. It has been around for so long that many gardeners have a nostalgia for bougainvillea just as we have a nostalgia for money plants (which also originate from somewhere else, the island of Mo'orea, next to Tahiti).

What I have noticed about non-native plants that do well here and become popular houseplants is that their price drops over time. The ZZ plant was very expensive when it first arrived as the 'YouTube' plant. But then gardens and nurseries started to grow and propagate their own ZZ plants, which they were able to sell at a lower price because they did not have to import them from overseas. In less than five years, the ZZ plant has become naturalized and is now much cheaper to buy and easier to take care of.

Be patient and pay less for plants

As plants become trendy online, you might see them sell for a high price at your local nursery. In the case of new, trendy plants, it is better *not* to be an early adopter unless you are willing to risk your money on a plant that might not do well in your home. What I advise is to wait a few years and see if the price drops. Is the plant doing well in India? If it becomes less expensive, it has probably naturalized. When growers are able to easily multiply a plant, they save money, and you save money, too.

Then again, there are some plants that come to India from another country and do so well here that they become invasive. For example, water hyacinths were introduced to India at the end of the eighteenth century as a gift from the British. These plants originated from the Amazon rainforest, where they grew along water basins. Soon after being introduced to India, water hyacinths invaded many of our water bodies, causing an imbalance, killing many fish and affecting the livelihood of fishermen (thanks a lot, Britain!).

Due to the invasive nature of plants like water hyacinths, many plants that come from outside India are regulated to make sure that they do not overtake the country, so you will not be able to find these plants at the nursery in the first place.

So what can we expect at the nursery? Let's take a trip. Pack your bags. We're going to the nursery.

5

Adopting a Plant: Preparing for Plant Parenthood

We know now that plants grow in a garden, nursery or forest, surrounded by other plants, receiving certain quantities of light, water and attention. We also know there are different kinds of plants with different characteristics, desires, superpowers and personalities. The best thing we can do to welcome our plants into our homes is ease them into our environment so that they feel less of a shock. Our job is to prevent our plants from feeling stressed. We should show them, 'Hey, I know what you like and what you are used to. I'm here to take care of you and make you feel at home.'

Before I go to the nursery, I prepare by taking notes about the light conditions in my home. I've lived in my home for a while now, so I have a lot of this information in my head. But if it's your first-time shopping for plants, you might want to walk around and get a good idea of the best places to keep plants in your home. It is much easier to find a plant that will grow well in our homes than it is to adapt our homes to the needs of our plants.

The people who work at the nursery do not know my space, my needs or the light situation in my house. If it is going to be a large plant, it needs plenty of space like an area on the floor or a balcony where it can stretch its limbs. Smaller plants may be able to sit on a sill or on a shelf.

Knowing where I want to keep my plant also gives me a good idea of how much light it will receive (frequency) and how bright the light will be (intensity).

When I am determining the intensity of light, I think about which direction my windows are facing. Generally, if you live in the northern hemisphere, the windows that face south will get the most direct sunlight throughout the day. If you live in the southern hemisphere, it is reversed with north-facing windows receiving the most direct sunlight. I use a compass app on my smartphone to figure out which way is south.

Light intensity is affected by many different factors such as how tinted your windows are, or whether or not there are trees or other objects that filter the light before it reaches your plant. For instance, if you have a dusty window, less light will shine through. It is a good idea to keep your windows clean and remove any dust to get a better idea of how much light your windowsill gets throughout the day.

Too much heat or too much cold can also damage your plant. Your plant's leaves can get a sunburn if it is in harsh light or hot temperatures that it is not meant to endure. Be careful to observe direct light, draughts from your window and the airflow from nearby fans and air-conditioning (AC) units. If you intend to keep your plant near a window, make sure it is well sealed, especially if you live in an area that has hot summers or freezing winters. Also, be aware of any draughts produced by your outdoor AC units. If you put your plants too close to an AC unit that is blowing hot air, its leaves may get burnt.

There is a simple test I use to determine how intense the light is in certain areas of my home using only a pen. You can learn more about the pen test and how to check the intensity of light in your home in the light section of this book. There's also some great information about soil and buying pots later in this book, so if you want to be fully prepared for going to the nursery, you might want to read the rest of this book first.

But if you already have some plants or went to the nursery, no need to worry. You will still find plenty of ways to apply this knowledge on your next visit. After all, gardening is a lifelong journey.

Preparing for the nursery

When we go to the nursery, it is easy to get carried away by all the plants, and then we forget about our home's environment. We might end up leaving the nursery with a begonia, a monstera and a succulent when we were really looking for something more like a snake plant that can live on a windowsill that gets a moderate amount of light.

So what can we do to stay on track? I like to take along some notes: where I am going to keep the plant, the light level and the ideal size.

You will notice that the one thing I do not list is the plant that I want to buy. It is healthier and more fulfilling to keep an open mind instead of going directly to the plant we saw online. Remember, if we go to the nursery looking for a specific plant

Preparing for the nursery

we saw on social media without knowing what we are getting into, we may end up buying one that is stressed, overpriced and outside its comfort zone.

Before I leave, I do the pen test on the window where I want to keep my new plant. My office window faces east, and the shadow cast by the pen during the middle of the day is slightly blurry and diffused, meaning that it gets a medium amount of light. Not too bright, but not too dim—perfect for a tropical plant that needs medium to bright light.

When should we plan to go to the nursery? I find that mornings are the best time to go. The earlier in the day you bring your new plants home, the more time they will have in the sunlight to adjust. If you bring a plant home at night, it will have nightmares! Just kidding. But plants do prefer to adjust with a full day of sunlight. Shopping in the morning and moving them to their new home in the light of day keeps your plants on their regular light cycle and makes it easier for them to feel at home.

We are now almost ready to go to the nursery and pick out our plants, but I want to grab a few more things before we go: a mat and some boxes. A gardening mat, *bori* (jute bags) or even some large towels are great to keep in your car, especially if you plan on buying a lot of plants. I like to lay them down over my seats to prevent dirt, leaves and debris from getting all over my car. Using a large piece of fabric also makes it easy to clean up any mess—simply grab the sheet by the corners, take it outside, flip it over and dust it.

Boxes secure your plants so they do not move around too much in your car. Plants may be tough, but we want to minimize stress as much as possible. They already underwent a long trip to get to the nursery; to show them that they are about to be moved to a more loving and welcoming home, it is good to give them a calm and relaxing trip. Like any good parent, make sure your kids are buckled up.

Boxes also make it easier to carry plants from your vehicle to your home. Sometimes I might buy a lot of plants, and after getting ready, going to the nursery, shopping for plants, carrying them to my car and driving home, the last thing I want to do is carry the plants inside one at a time. But I never leave the plants in my car because it gets too hot for them in there and deprives them of oxygen. This is not the time to be lazy. You need to bring the kids inside.

When I have a box, it is easy to pick up all my plants at once and make a single trip from my car to their new home. I typically keep cardboard boxes in my car just in case I get the urge to go plant shopping, but in planned situations, I double-check to make sure I have some boxes with me before I go buy plants. One easy way to spot an active plant parent is to see if they have boxes in their cars with loose dirt in them.

Now that we have our notes, our bori and our boxes, we are ready to go shopping!

Choosing a plant

Your first trip to the nursery might be overwhelming. Where can I find the best plants? What if I get lost in the ficus plants? What if I have questions? Whom should I ask?

Don't worry. Today, I will take you along and help you answer these questions.

The first thing you will notice as we enter the nursery is the layout. Most nurseries have a similar set-up. Usually towards the front is a large outdoor area with plants that are out in the sun. Here in the sun is where you'll find blooming wonders, storage houses and other plants that flourish and thrive in bright light. Then there is usually a covered area with a green net canopy for plants that need shade. Under this net is where you are likely to find wanderers and other canopy plants that enjoy low-to-medium light. Stiff and sterns such as lemon trees, figs and rose plants need a lot of light but also like to keep cool and avoid direct sunlight so they don't get burnt. They are often found at the edge of the covered areas, or in the spaces between the bright and covered areas.

Today, we are looking for a couple of plants to keep inside and a couple of plants to keep out on the balcony. Let's try to find one of each type of plant: a storage house, a wanderer, a blooming wonder, and a stiff and stern.

We're going to start with wanderers, which are good to keep on a low-light windowsill. So let's head straight to the covered area. Shaded areas like these can vary from nursery to nursery, and some larger nurseries may have multiple shaded areas, or indoor areas with varying degrees of shade.

Shaded and open spaces in nurseries

What happens if you are shopping for a low-light plant and get a plant from the bright, sunlit, outdoor area? When you bring that plant home and put it inside, it is not going to be happy and will probably not survive. If that plant was well suited for shade, the nursery would have put it in the shade in the first place. There are some species of plants, like the snake plant, that can do well in either shade or direct sunlight, but it would be cruel to take a plant that is used to bright, direct sunlight and put it in a shaded area devoid of the sunlight it needs to thrive. It is just as cruel to put a low-light plant in direct, intense sunlight. If you are going to buy a plant from the outdoor area, make sure you keep it outside.

On our way to the shaded area, we run into my old pal Ashok who has helped me shop for the right plant before. It is good to befriend the people who work at your local nursery.

They are there to help, and they know a lot about the plants at the nursery. They are like their foster parents.

Not all plants in the shaded area receive the same amount of shade, though. The edge of the shaded area will get some sunlight spilling into it from outside the net. A plant from the edge may be happy if it is going to live next to a bright window or on the balcony, but if I want a plant that is going to live on my low-light windowsill, I have to go deeper into the shaded area to find one that is acclimated to low light. Good thing we did the pen test!

I go deeper into the covered area and find a few rows of syngoniums. Some of them have torn leaves and stems pressed against each other—maybe they just got here from a long truck ride. But many of the syngoniums in this area have big, green healthy leaves and stems coming out, which are signs of new growth and a happy plant. I am curious to know when these plants arrived at the nursery, so I ask Ashok, 'When did these syngoniums get here?' He tells me that some came in last week, and the others came a month ago. It makes sense now why some of them seem more acclimated than others.

The potted syngonium plants are lined up on the ground in eight rows and four columns. Which row should we select our plant from? Should we choose one from the middle rows, or the periphery? A younger Vinayak would have gone for the plants in the middle. Surely these plants have been touched less and have been there longer, right?

Actually, what I have found is that the plants on the periphery are bushier and usually have better overall growth because they receive light from more directions. The plants in the middle receive light only from the top, so they only grow upwards instead of outwards. Many gardeners refer to plants that only grow upwards as 'leggy', and avoid them because they grow less flowers, branches and fruit than bushy plants do.

Now it is time for us to pick out which of these lucky plants is coming home with me. Always pay attention to the foundation of the plant. Just as with a house, the foundation will determine how sturdy the plant is, and how well it will stand the test of time. Many new plant shoppers look at the leaves, which makes sense because leaves are often the most eye-catching part of the plant. For instance, a monstera's leaves are large and resemble Swiss cheese. When we see a wilted or dry leaf, we may think, 'Oh no! This plant is sad!'

But I suggest that we do not pay too much attention to the leaves when first picking out a plant. Older leaves are naturally going to wither as new leaves grow. It is true that a sad-looking leaf is a sign that a plant is stressed, but it is common to see yellow or wilted leaves in a nursery; these plants are acclimating and making way for new growth. The plant will grow new leaves if it is well taken care of.

While leaves may tell us how happy a plant is at the present moment, the secret to a successful future is held in its roots and stems. If I compare two syngoniums and find that one pot has three stems coming out of the soil as opposed to a single stem, I'll choose the one with three stems.

I have now found a nice, healthy syngonium with multiple stems growing those pretty, patterned leaves that syngoniums are known for. But there's one last thing I want to look at: the roots. I pick up the pot, look underneath and notice that the roots are coming out of the bottom of the pot.

Should I be worried? I do not think so. In fact, I am thrilled.

Even though the roots coming out of the pot indicate that it is root-bound, I now know for sure that this syngonium is ready to be moved to a bigger pot. Sometimes you might even notice roots coming out of the top of the pot, which indicates the same thing: that it is ready for a slightly bigger pot. In a way, I am getting an even better deal because I'm buying a large plant for the price of a medium-sized one. It is like getting two sookha (dry) puris with your golgappa, pani puri or puchka!

Now let's try to find a nice stiff and stern. We go to the edge of the covered area and see a row of lemon trees. Great! My balcony could use a nice lemon tree. But which one should we choose?

You'll notice that the taller, more fully grown lemon trees are more expensive because they've had time to grow under the care of the nursery. If you're patient, you pay less. Today, I want a lemon tree that has some growth, but still needs some time to mature. It's spring, so none of the lemon trees are producing lemons.

So how can we tell which of these lemon trees will grow to produce a lot of lemons? I look at the branches.

Branching takes time, and plants will not branch until they reach a certain age. If you see a stiff and stern with many branches, and every other branch is also branching, that is a good sign that it's going to bear more fruit, flowers or leaves. Whatever you want from that stiff and stern, branches will give you more of it.

The tricky part is finding a stiff and stern that isn't fully mature but has started to branch just enough that we can tell that it will be a fruitful purchase. I find a young lemon tree that has quite a few new branches and bring it along with my syngonium.

Just outside the covered area, I see a table with snake plants on it. Snake plants are good storage houses for beginners because they're easy to take care of and look great in almost any room. We are looking to get a good deal, so let's try to avoid the tall, fully-grown snake plants.

How do we find a baby snake plant that is likely to give us a lot of growth? We look at the pups. Pups are the small buds that peek out from the soil, indicating where a cluster of snake plant leaves will grow. Similar to how we looked for multiple stems and branches, looking for multiple pups in a pot is a good way to tell that we're going to get more snake plants from a single pot.

Like many other storage houses, snake plants self-propagate, which means they'll produce new pups as long as they're healthy. We might see a pot that has a few clusters of longer leaves and a few new pups peeking out from the soil. We see a pot that has two clusters of leaves that are already grown, and two pups poking out. That's like getting two young plants and two baby plants in one pot! This is the snake plant I want, so I grab it and introduce it to its soon-to-be roommates, the syngonium and the lemon tree.

Finally, I want to add some beauty to my house, so I look for a nice blooming wonder. We don't have to go far, though, because we're already in the bright area of the nursery and nearby is another table with plenty of sadabahar. Once again, I want to find a younger sadabahar that will one day grow plenty of flowers. The good thing is that it's spring, so we can see flowers on these sadabahar. Sadabahar are perennial plants, so they will live throughout the year, and might also blossom again in the fall. Even if it wasn't spring, we would be looking for a sadabahar with many stems based on the assumption that more stems equates to more potential flowers. I find a nice, young sadabahar that is beginning to blossom several beautiful flowers and decide that this is the one. I'm excited to bring it home with the rest of my plants and watch it fully bloom.

I grab a couple of extra pots, chat with Ashok for a few minutes and pay for the plants. I pack the plants and pots in the boxes in my car so that they don't move around and buckle them in for the ride home.

As you can see, I do take the time to shop around and look at the plants, but I try not to overthink it. If you have questions, ask someone at the nursery. And remember that these plants will have plenty of time to grow under our care, so we don't always need to buy the biggest, most mature plant at the nursery. In fact, I advise that new gardeners start with a baby plant so that it can grow along with you as you grow as a gardener.

6

Welcoming Your Plants to Your Home

When we first bring plants home, they feel disoriented and need time to get used to their new surroundings and roommates. We are moving them into our houses, apartments and offices to make us feel more at home and to appreciate their beauty. But while plants improve our lives, it is just as important to remember to make them feel at home and improve their lives, too. After all, plants want to survive and be happy, just like us.

For the plant, coming to a new home is like visiting another country or moving to a new city. When I lived in Lyon, France as an exchange student, it took me some time to overcome culture shock. I had to adjust my diet to French cuisine and learn my way around the city. I did not know anyone other than the students I had come with. At home, I feel comfortable because I know my way around and how to talk to people, but in France, I felt uneasy because I was not always sure if I was saying the right thing or going in the right direction.

Some of the other Indian students and I ended up finding a Moroccan community with restaurants that served couscous and moussaka, which reminded us of home. It was always nice to meet someone from India because they understood the challenges we had as Indian students visiting France. We were all anxious about taking the subway because it was foreign to us, but we loved exploring Lyon on our bicycles, which is how we would travel around campus back home.

Just like anyone visiting a new place, it will take time for your plants to become familiar with your home. For the plant, it's like a foreign country! This doesn't necessarily mean that we need to be overprotective. Plants have a survival instinct; they won't instantly fall apart when moved to a new place, but they will show us if they're not happy by changing colours, wilting and losing leaves. As a plant parent, we need to be mindful and pay attention to what our plants are trying to tell us.

There are things that we can do to minimize the stress that our plants feel and make them feel at home. As your plants adjust, they will find things to love about their new home, and if you care for your plants throughout their lives, they will love you, too.

When I bring plants home, I like to keep them in the same pot they were in when I picked them out at the nursery for at least a couple of weeks. Their roots are familiar with that soil. Even in the case of my new syngonium, which has roots hanging out of the bottom of the pot, I don't want to move it to a new pot immediately. I want to give it some time to adjust to its new home and get used to my place. Remember, it is our job to minimize any stress that our plants feel, and for the plant, moving from the nursery to my home is like moving from India to France for me. It's going to need some time to acclimate.

You may have noticed that I *did not* get my plants repotted at the nursery. Some nurseries offer to repot your new plants, but I strongly recommend that you wait and do it yourself. Even though I'm in no hurry to repot my new plants, I will eventually want to move them into slightly larger pots so they have a chance to spread their roots and grow. Not only is repotting your plants going to make them feel more at ease but it will also be a good chance for you to get your hands dirty. I'll cover repotting later in this book.

I'm also careful not to put my new plants next to my old plants for the first couple of weeks. Although it's unlikely, sometimes plants we get from the nursery can have pests or diseases that spread to other plants. I definitely don't want that to happen. By keeping them quarantined, I can observe them and make sure that they aren't carrying anything that could harm my other plants.

I learnt this lesson the hard way a while back. I was driving down the road and saw some pretty flowers that looked like sunflowers. I dug one up, put it in a pot that I had in my car and brought it home. I put it on my balcony next to my other plants. Within ten days or so, almost all the plants on my balcony were eaten by insects.

I learnt two lessons: don't pick random plants from the side of the road, and don't bring your new plants into an area where any insects they may be hosting can destroy your whole garden. While plants from a nursery are safer than plants you might find on the side of the road, snails, ants and other stowaways can hide in the soil, and many diseases spread slowly and are hard to notice when you're shopping for plants.

Even though I intend to put my new syngonium on my office desk, I might keep it on my shaded balcony by itself for the first couple of weeks. But don't worry. I'll check in on it so that it doesn't get lonely.

When is a good time to repot your plants and move them inside? As soon as you see new growth, it means your plant is stress-free and happy in its new home. You may notice some of the older leaves turning yellow or brown, but that is no reason to be alarmed. Just like at the nursery, the plant is adjusting to its new home, so you can expect some of the older leaves to show signs of stress. As long as you see new growth, your plant is happy.

The next day, I check the soil of each of my new plants to see if it is dry, and then I give them a thorough watering. I like to water my plants in the morning because then they have the daytime for the soil to dry and prevent the roots from rotting. I also like to water new plants fairly soon after bringing them home because the soil moves around when they are being transported, and watering them is a good way to fill in any air pockets that were created around the roots.

For the next few weeks, I am going to check on my syngonium, my snake plant, my lemon tree and my sadabahar. When I see some new growth (and confirm that they don't have bugs or diseases), I will repot them. Once I see that the snake plant and syngonium have new growth after being moved to their new pots, I'll bring them inside to join their new friends on my desk. And I'll keep my lemon tree and sadabahar out on the patio with my herb plants.

Recap: Adopting plants from the nursery

We want to minimize stress for plants so they feel happy and survive.

Before you go plant shopping:

- Think about where you want to keep the plant
- Measure the light level
- Take notes
- Pack a sheet and some boxes

While shopping:

- Go to the area with a light level that matches that in your home (refer to your notes)
- Look for new growth
- Look at the stems, branches and roots

Bringing plants home:

- Keep away from other plants for at least two weeks
- Water when soil is dry
- Wait for new growth before repotting and moving to where you intend to keep it

Part II

What Your Plants Need to
Live and Be Happy

So far we have discussed why plants are important and how they enrich our life. But as plant parents, we must remember that plants live their own lives. And like any good parent we must ask ourselves: what do our plant babies need to be happy?

You probably already know that plants need light, water and soil. But how much light? When should we give them water? What soil should we use?

Just as with our health, the details matter. For example, we need food and water to survive. But that does not mean we can live by eating only parathas for breakfast, lunch and dinner while drinking water from the River Ganga! I will admit that I enjoy some tasty street food every once in a while, but in order to live a long, happy, healthy life, it is best to eat your veggies and drink plenty of water.

Of course, plants are different from humans in one big way: they make their own food. So while you may never see a plant chow down on a samosa, it is important to understand that the light and water we give them and the soil we put them in are what they use to make food within their cells.

Because each plant has adapted to different environments by growing different types of leaves, roots and stems, we can look at our plants to figure out how much water and light they prefer and the type of soil they want to live in. In the following sections, we will learn what to look for in our plants to determine the amount and quality of water, light, soil and nutrients that will allow them to live happy, healthy lives.

We start with the process that ties together all the things that plants love: photosynthesis.

Photosynthesis: How plants make their own food

I try to teach gardeners how to intuitively understand their plants' needs. For example, if the leaves look dry, is it time for water? Or does the plant need less light?

How plants prepare their food

Knowing how photosynthesis works is the building block for us to answer these questions. When we know how plants make food, we can make better decisions for their well-being.

Photosynthesis is what separates plants from all other life. It allows them to make their own food with just water, light and air—making plants the foundation of our entire food chain. All life depends on plants!

Essentially, every plant is its own chef. The ingredients it needs are carbon dioxide (CO2) and water. But just as we need a little heat from our stove to cook our food, plants need light to photosynthesize the carbon dioxide and water. The word 'photosynthesis' comes from the Greek word 'photo', for 'light', and 'synthesis', which means 'put together'.

Plants take in light and carbon dioxide through their leaves. They can regulate how much CO2 they take in through little valve-like pores on the surface of each leaf. These pores are called 'stomas'.

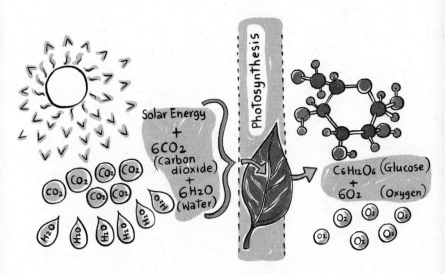

The process of photosynthesis

Plants use their roots to take in water and other nutrients from the soil. In turn, they produce glucose (sugar) and oxygen. So while the leaves are breathing in CO2 and the roots are slurping up water, the plant can get to cooking.

You may be wondering, 'What about soil? Don't plants need soil, too?' It's a good observation. Soil plays a large role in giving the plant some structure so that it can have easy access to water and carbon dioxide, as well as other nutrients that help it make food more efficiently. So while soil isn't an ingredient that a plant needs to make food, it does help it get those ingredients.

From now on, when we're making decisions for our plants—where to keep them, when to give them water, and what pots and soil to keep them in—I want us to always consider photosynthesis.

1

Light

Of all the things plants need to be happy, light is the element that most impacts what kind of plants we get and where we keep them. Plants take in light through any green part of their body. If there's green, that typically means there is chlorophyll, which is the pigment chemical within the chloroplast that absorbs light. Think of chloroplast as an energy generator—it takes in solar (light) energy, and then uses it to convert CO_2 and water into food for the plant.

There are two ways we can control how much light our plants receive. We can control how bright the light is, and we can control how long the light shines on our plants. Of course, light is not tangible like water. We can't simply gather some light and pour it on our plants. So adjusting how much light our plants get typically involves physically moving our plants or finding ways to filter light, either through shade or by controlling the light source.

Finding the right light for your plants

When we are deciding where to keep our plants, it's important to think about the light in each area of our homes, as well as how that light may change throughout the day and during different seasons. In India, the sun shines bright, direct light in the summers and less intense light in the winters. As a general rule, south-facing windows receive the most light (if you're in the northern hemisphere).

Measuring the light in different parts of your home doesn't require any fancy equipment. All you need is a pen.

The Pen Test

Using a pen to determine light intensity

Step 1: Find a pen or any similarly shaped object that is tall and thin.

Step 2: Bring the pen to the area where you want to test the light. You may want to do the pen test at different times of the day.

Step 3: Place one end of the pen on a surface and place your finger on the other end of the pen so that it stands tall and casts a shadow.

Step 4: Look at the shadow. How dark is it? How defined are its edges? More defined edges and darker shadows means brighter light.

Bright light = Well-defined shadow
Medium light = Blurry, diffused shadow
Low light = No defined shadow

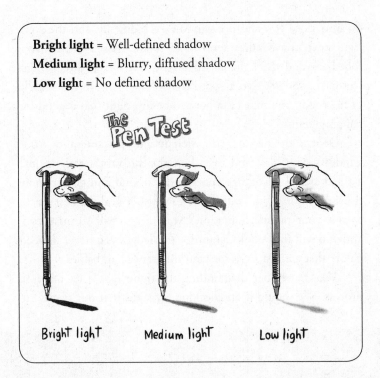

As I'm doing the pen test in different areas, I like to open my curtains and walk around, seeing how the light casts shadows. If I plan on putting plants on the ground, I may even crouch down and use a pen to see how bright the sun's rays are on the floor. I walk around during the morning and test the light, then test it again at noon, in the afternoon, and when the sun is setting. If you do this exercise in your home, you will notice that as the sun moves through the sky, the light will move across your walls and floors, adjusting in intensity at different locations throughout the day.

Another thing you'll notice as you pay more attention to the light in each room is that the light varies in intensity depending on how close you are to a window. Windowsills and the areas right next to a window tend to catch the most light. Move a foot back and the light is still bright, but not as direct. Four feet back, and we start to get bright shade. And in the middle of the room, you may even have some low light that is good for hanging plants.

Depending on the size, height and placement of your windows, you may find that the light can vary greatly in just a small area. I encourage you to play around and get to know the light throughout your home so you can find the best places to put your plants. Sometimes your home will surprise you, and you will find nooks, crannies and ledges you never noticed before that are just right for your different plant babies.

Also, remember that finding the right light is an ongoing process. We should keep checking for signs that our plants are

The different areas around a home, showing varying degrees of light intensity

happy, and if they seem to be getting too much or too little light, we can move them as needed.

Low-light plants that are happy inside

All plants will do better in more light, but not all plants like heat. Remember, sunlight is light *and* heat. Just as we can get a sunburn, the sun's intense light can make our plants too toasty. In nature, larger plants can protect other plants from the sun's harsh rays. The canopy of a rainforest, for example, filters the sun's light so that it does not burn the plants that grow underneath. Many of these plants that live in the filtered light of the rainforest—such as syngonium, pothos and monstera—are the same plants that do well inside our homes.

Some people might call these plants 'indoor plants', but as I mentioned earlier, I think the term 'indoor' is misleading since they are actually from the rainforest. They just happen to do well indoors. I prefer to call these plants 'low-light plants' because that's what they are: plants that can live in lower light conditions.

But we typically do not buy our plants directly from the rainforest; we purchase them from a nursery or we may get a clipping from the community park or a fellow plant lover. So it is important that we consider both the species of our plant and the experience of the individual plant. For example, we know syngonium is from the Amazon rainforest, so naturally syngoniums enjoy shaded light. But if you go to the nursery and pick a syngonium that has spent time in bright shade, it may have a slightly higher tolerance for warm light than a syngonium that was raised in deeper, darker shade.

One advantage of buying plants at the nursery is that you can see where the plant has lived some of its life, whether it's in a shaded area or in the direct sun. You can also get a sense of the kind of light your plant likes by learning where that species of plant originated. Did it come from the ground floor of the rainforest? Then it probably enjoys shade. Did it come from the desert? Then it might enjoy brighter light.

Low-light plants that do well inside:

Money plant (pothos)
Snake plant
Spider plant
Syngonium
Philodendrons
Aglaonema
ZZ plant

Rotating plants for even growth

Have you ever seen a plant that looks lopsided, with all the leaves and growth going in one direction? If you have a lopsided plant, you may wonder how to encourage the leaves and stems to grow out evenly in all directions. The trick is to ensure that all the leaves receive a balanced amount of light.

Unless you live in a glass house or have a greenhouse, chances are that only one side of your plant receives sunlight. For instance, I keep my plants near a window, which is great for the side of the plant facing the window, but what about the other side of the plant? What I see is the leaves all growing in one direction: towards the light.

If we want our plants to grow on all sides but only have one window to work with, we can rotate our plants so that each side gets light throughout the week. What I like to do is rotate my plants 180 degrees every Sunday. Now, instead of all the leaves and stems reaching in one direction, I find that my plants have nice, even growth.

Moving plants inside and outside

Many plant parents wonder: is it okay to take my low-light plants outside? I know for me, when it is a nice day, I want to go outside and feel the breeze and the sun, and I think, 'I want my plants to feel how nice it is outside!' In most cases, it is good to give the plants you keep inside some outdoor time.

Before you take them outside, check to see how harsh the sun is. Is it overcast? Or is the light beating down on my balcony? If it is too hot and sunny, I may not want to take my pilea outside, because its beautiful, round leaves are likely to get burnt. But if it is cloudy, or I have some shade on my balcony, I may take it outside to sit in the shaded sun for the day.

I recommend taking your plants outside every week or two so that they can get some extra light, which will help them make more food. It is like taking your plant to an all-you-can-eat buffet! And while your plants are outside, you can use this opportunity to water them so you can avoid making a mess inside. But we still need to be careful not to put these plants in direct sunlight, so keep your low-light plants in a shaded area of your balcony.

As you become more experienced and begin to care for more plants, you can experiment with keeping some plants outside and some plants inside for longer periods, and then switching them. Always be mindful of what the weather is like outside, and never leave your plants out in extremely hot or cold temperatures.

How to tell if your plant is getting too much or too little light?

There are several ways to tell if your plant needs more or less light. But remember, water *and* light are both required for photosynthesis, so sometimes it is not just the light that needs fixing, but also the ratio of water to light.

If your plant has brown, crunchy leaves that look like they are burnt, it is probably in light that is too hot. Try moving your plant to the shade, and make sure to give it a thorough watering if the soil is thoroughly dry.

If your plant is droopy or shrivelled up, but not burnt, then it may not be getting enough light, or may be getting too much water. Make sure that water can drain from the bottom of the pot, and that your plant does not have root rot, and then try moving it to a brighter area.

Lighting methods: Natural light versus lamps

All light is good for plants. Sunlight is one of the best types of light that plants can get. But as I mentioned before, the problem with sunlight is that it can sometimes be too hot.

Incandescent, LED and fluorescent lights all emit enough energy to be useful to plants, but the light they emit is less intense than sunlight. You can purchase grow lights that are optimized to emit a broad spectrum of light similar to the sun. The problem with grow lights is that while they are great for helping our plants, they are not the best lights for humans to stare at or be around. In fact, grow lights are disorientating for most people. Walking into a room lit only by grow lamps makes my head hurt. Grow lamps are great if you have a dedicated place for gardening that you do not have to spend a lot of time inside, but it defeats the purpose if you want to spend time with your plants.

Almost any light you have inside your home—bulbs, lamps, tube lights, etc.—will help your plant grow. You can help your plant even more by moving it closer to these lights and increasing the amount of time you keep them on.

Recap: Photosynthesis and light

Plants use light as an energy source during photosynthesis to turn water and CO_2 into food.

Plants need light to use water.

If your plant has droopy leaves, it may be overwatered or not receiving enough light. Move it to a brighter area.

Different plants prefer more or less light depending on where they originate, and what conditions they were in while growing at the nursery.

Plants that originate from the canopy of a rainforest, such as wanderers, prefer indirect light, while plants that originate from bright desert areas, such as storage houses, prefer direct light. Likewise, plants from a bright area of a nursery prefer bright light, while plants from a shaded area prefer shaded light.

You can use a pen to test varying light intensities around your home.

Light also transmits heat.

While all plants enjoy light, many plants can be burnt by heat. Be careful not to leave your plants in bright, direct sunlight when it is too hot. If your plant has burnt leaves, it may be receiving too much bright direct light or be too hot. Move it to a more shaded area.

Leaves and stems tend to grow towards light.

If you have plants near a window, you can rotate them so that each side grows evenly. You can also move plants that you keep inside your home to your balcony on nice days so that they can enjoy some extra sunlight.

All light is good for plants.

While sunlight is one of the best sources of light for plants, they can also use the light emitted from lightbulbs around your home for photosynthesis.

2

Water

Water is probably the most misunderstood component of plant care. As we learnt in our discussion of photosynthesis, water is a key ingredient plants need to make food. Plants need water to stay alive, just like us. So when we see a plant that looks sad, droopy or shrivelled, our first instinct is to give it water.

But sometimes water is not the answer. In fact, many plants die because they are given *too much* water, which leads to root rot. Root rot is a catch-all term for any disease or fungus that plants' roots develop from sitting in water for extended periods of time.

Just like every plant has its own preferences when it comes to light, every plant prefers different amounts of water. Storage houses originate from arid environments and only need water once every few months, while wanderers originate from tropical environments and may need to be watered every week. There are only a few plants that want to be watered every day, and even then, it depends on the season, the soil and the drainage system of the pot. Remember: plants and soil can retain water, so even when we're not giving them water, they probably have some leftover in their soil, leaves and roots to keep making food.

We know that plants take in light through their leaves, but how do they take in water? Through their roots.

Roots: What your plants use to drink water

When we look at plants, we see the leaves and the flowers, and that's what we often care about the most. We all want our plants to look pretty above the surface! But all that depends on the roots beneath the soil.

Your plant's roots have three jobs:

1) Keep the plant stable
2) Seek out water
3) Absorb water

Roots are living tissue, and they breathe just like you and me. If their soil is always saturated in water, they can become suffocated, and root rot can set in. If you've ever seen a plant propagating in water or grown hydroponically, you might be wondering why those plants don't develop root rot. We will discuss why in the propagation section.

Just as leaves and stems grow towards the light, roots can sense moisture and will try to grow in that direction. Whereas leaves and stems grow upward towards the light, roots are pulled down by gravity and grow downward.

There are three parts of the root system: the primary root, secondary roots and tertiary roots. The primary root, also called a 'taproot', is directly attached to the stem of your plant and goes straight down into the soil, like a drill digging for water.

As soon as the primary root detects water, it will split off into secondary roots. Secondary roots, also known as 'radial roots', spread outwards from the taproot, seeking water in all directions. If these roots encounter a lot of moisture, they may split up again into tertiary roots.

What happens to the water that we give our plants?

When we water our plants, four things happen to the water:

1) Some of the water simply drains out the bottom of the pot
2) Some of it evaporates from the soil into the air
3) Some of it is released by the leaves through transpiration
4) Some of it is used by the plant to make food through photosynthesis

For a well-potted plant, a lot of the water will soak through the soil and out of the drainage system.

The hotter the environment is, the faster the water will evaporate from the soil. If you keep your plant outside in the sun after watering, more water will evaporate.

Transpiration helps plants cool down and facilitates the movement of nutrients and minerals throughout the plant. Essentially, transpiration is when water passes back out of the leaves through the stomas, or the small pores on the leaf. How fast or slow plants transpire water depends on the structure of the plant and the humidity in the air—the drier the air, the more your plant will transpire. You'll notice that succulents and cacti typically don't have leaves, and if they do, they are hard and waxy, making it easier to store water by reducing transpiration. Other storage houses might store water in their leaves or underground in rhizomes or taproots. A rhizome is an overgrown underground plant stem that is thickened by deposits of water and food material. It produces shoots above and roots below.

The water that is not lost through drainage and evaporation is sucked up by the roots, travels through the stem and finally into the leaves where it is combined with CO_2 and light to make food.

How often should I water my plants?

I sometimes think about photosynthesis when I prepare my morning tea. I like to drink my tea with milk. If I run out of milk, I often do not drink tea.

Plants are similar. If they don't get light, they won't use water, which is one reason why plants need less water in the winter months when the days are shorter.

How often you water your plant depends on how much light your plant receives. The more light your plant gets, the faster it will photosynthesize, and the faster excess water will evaporate from the soil.

Now let's consider plants that we keep inside. They get less light than the plants we keep outside, so they will use less water for photosynthesis. The further into the shade we place a plant, the less water it will need. The bottom line is: plants need light to use water.

So how can we use this knowledge to help an overwatered plant? We could repot it and move it to drier soil, but that is tedious, messy and stressful for the plant. Most of the time, the best solution is to move it to a brighter area.

So how often should we water our plants? Daily? Weekly?

It's a trick question. There is no fixed schedule. How often we water our plants depends on the type of plant, the season, how bright the light has been, how dry the air is, when we watered it last, how much we watered it and how fast the water drains from the pot. Instead of asking 'How often?' we should ask, 'How do I know when my plants are thirsty?'

I like to compare it to my sleep schedule. I try to wake up at 6. 30 a.m., but some days if I didn't get a good night's sleep or if I worked late into the night, I might want to sleep in. Plants are the same way. Their needs change.

Okay, maybe not exactly the same. My plants work a little harder than I do.

How do I know when my plants need water?

The best way to know if your plants need more water is to check whether or not the soil is completely dry. If there is still any moisture in the soil, do not add new water. It is best to wait because then the roots have the opportunity to stretch and grow and find the water deep in the soil. If water is always easy for the roots to access, they will not have any incentive to grow as long as they would in nature.

I use my finger to check how dry the soil is. All I do is take my pointer finger, push it an inch into the soil and see if any sticks. If the soil sticks, it means that there is still water in the soil. If there is any wet soil on the top layer, there is definitely going to be water in the layers beneath. So if the soil sticks to your finger, do not water. More plants are killed from overwatering than anything else. Don't let that be your plant.

So what about the reverse? If the soil doesn't stick to your finger, does it mean you should water it? Maybe. But I would

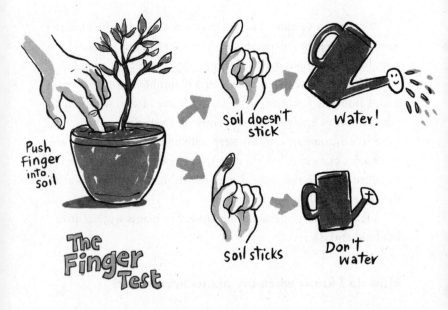

The Finger Test

Push finger into soil

Soil doesn't stick → Water!

Soil sticks → Don't water

still use my discretion and experience. Typically, if I notice that the top layer of soil is dry, I will still wait three or four days before watering it.

Overwatering is more dangerous for plants than underwatering.

Once you familiarize yourself with your plant babies, you won't need to put your finger into the soil every time you water your plants. You will learn how often they like water and what they look like when they are thirsty.

Most plants are designed to store water and survive dry spells in nature. In fact, many plants enjoy dry spells in between watering, especially storage houses.

Letting your plants' roots dry has three benefits:

1) It allows roots to search for water and grow deeper into the soil
2) It lets roots breathe
3) It prevents root rot by keeping away unnecessary diseases

Think about food that becomes mouldy. You've probably learnt that it's better to store food in a dry area, or to dry out vegetables and fruit before storing them in a plastic bag so that they don't attract mould. The same concept applies to roots. If our plants' roots are always wet, they're either going to rot, become infected or develop mould. Waiting a little longer to water after you notice the top layer of soil is dry is a good way to prevent root rot; it gives the roots the time they need to dry.

Here's an example from my own gardening practice. I have a snake plant and a ZZ plant that I haven't watered in a month. I notice that the soil is bone-dry. Still, I will wait a week to water them and they will be fine. I even notice that there is new growth on both plants, so I know that they're happy.

In many cases, watering plants is a lesson in patience. It's tempting to give our plants water or do something to stimulate growth. But plants take their time to drink and grow. We need to give them that time and space, and in turn, we learn how to wait and appreciate the time it takes for growth to happen.

Knowing when it is time to water our plants is essential to our gardening knowledge. However, it is also essential to know how to properly water our plants when we are sure they need a drink.

How to water your plants?

How you water your plant is going to affect the growth of the roots. When our plants have long, happy, healthy roots, they absorb more minerals and water, become more efficient at making energy, and grow into large, lovely plants. A strong foundation of roots at the bottom is vital to support a larger plant on top. If you don't encourage the roots to grow deep into the soil, your plant may think, 'If I get any bigger, I'll topple over!' and stop growing.

You may think that because overwatering is bad, it is better to give your plants only a little bit of water at a time. But root rot doesn't occur because we give our plants too much water at once; it happens when we always keep the soil wet. So it is actually better to wait longer between waterings. And when we do water our plants, it's best to water them thoroughly.

Think about when it rains. The sky opens up, and the rain pours until everything is wet. The average rainfall here in India is thirty to sixty centimetres, and during the monsoon season, hundreds of centimetres of rain can fall from the sky. That's a lot of water!

Plants are used to their roots being thoroughly watered when it rains, so we want to give our plants the same kind of experience at home. When you water your plants, make sure that the water drains all the way through the soil and out of the drain holes at the bottom of the pot. If we only water the top of the soil, the layers of soil underneath will harden and compress, which will mess up the drainage system and lead to root rot.

The benefit to watering all the soil is that it encourages our plants' roots to grow long and spread throughout the pot.

Roots naturally seek out water, so the more evenly the water is dispersed, the more evenly the roots will expand, creating a solid foundation and healthy root system. When we water all the soil, there is going to be moisture deep down in the pot that gives the roots a reason to grow.

A thorough watering also means we don't have to water our plants as often. As I mentioned earlier, I couldn't water the plants at my office for six weeks during the COVID-19 lockdown. But since I water my plants so thoroughly, when I finally reunited with my plant babies, I saw that they were all still growing. They were a little shocked, but happy to see me.

Thoroughly watering our plants also gives us a chance to test their drainage system. Are the holes at the bottom of the pot clogged? If the water isn't coming out of the bottom of the pot in a steady stream, then they probably are. You may need to break up the soil at the bottom of the pot, or repot the plant into a pot with a layer of gravel at the bottom to prevent the soil from compressing and clogging the hole.

You may also want to keep your plants outside for a day or two after you water them, especially if you have plants like the snake plant and the syngonium that can get root rot if they sit in wet soil for too long. The advantage to keeping your plants outside after you water them is that they will use the water much faster, and the roots will dry out quicker.

Because we are watering our plants until the water goes all the way through the drainage holes, things will get messy. I recommend taking your potted plants outside or onto your balcony to water them so you don't get your floors wet, but you can always water your plants over a sink, tub or gardening mat, too.

Watering plants from the bottom

Another less common method for watering plants is to place your potted plant in a tub of water so that water soaks through the bottom of the soil. This method is good for plants with deep roots, like cacti, that naturally pull water from deep underground because they do not receive a lot of rainwater.

To water from the bottom, you have to fill a tub until the water level is almost the height of the pot. This method only works if your pot has an excellent drainage system so that the water can flow up through the holes when it is submerged in water, and so that the water drains out of the bottom when you take the plant out of the tub.

If you have a well-draining soil and pot, you can water from either the top or the bottom. Plants from the rainforest, such as money plants, typically prefer to be watered from the top of the soil.

Water the soil, not the plant

Our goal when we water our plants is to get the water near the roots. The roots are what plants use to drink the water. They do not take in water through any other parts. In fact, some parts of plants don't like to get wet at all and can rot if they stay wet for too long. The part of the plant above the soil, including the stems, branches and leaves, is called the 'crown'. If moisture becomes trapped anywhere on the crown, it can develop a fungus that eats at the plant—a condition known as 'crown rot'.

Snake plants, spider plants, succulents and any other plant with flower-like or bird's nest-like structures tend to be more vulnerable to crown rot because there are more areas where water can become trapped.

So how do we water our plants without getting water on the leaves and stems? What I recommend is to use a bottle or watering can with a narrow spout to direct the water under the leaves, stems and branches, directly into the soil. We also need to water our plants evenly, so pour some of the water on one side of the soil, stop, turn the pot and water another side. Keep repeating until you've watered all around the plant, and water is draining through the bottom of the pot.

What happens if we don't water our plants evenly? They will not grow evenly in all directions.

Remember that roots support our plants, so if your plant is only supported on one side, you'll notice that it will start to lean, and might even topple over and fall out of the pot. The same concept applies to fertilizer sticks. If you use fertilizer sticks, make sure to place them evenly around the pot to promote even growth in the roots. If you have a small four-inch pot, one fertilizer stick is fine, but if your pot is any larger, make sure that they are evenly spaced. It is a good idea to water directly over the fertilizer sticks so that those nutrients can sink into the soil and be absorbed by your plant.

The main exception to this rule of 'water the soil, not the plant' is for wanderers where we want to mist the aerial roots so that we encourage them to grow.

Tap water versus filtered water

Many gardeners, including myself, use tap water to water our plants. While tap water will not kill your plants, it can leave salt deposits and other residue in the soil and on the pot.

But there is a good source of filtered water in most homes: your AC drain water. The water that drains from your AC was pulled from the air through condensation, so it is completely safe to use for watering your plants—sometimes better than tap water. It is also a great way to conserve water for drinking and cleaning.

You can also collect rainwater by setting jars, buckets or barrels outside when it rains. You may even want to leave your plants out in the rain. Just make sure that the plants outside have a good drainage system so that the water does not gather on top of the soil.

Do not **water your plants with wastewater from a reverse osmosis (RO) water filter.** RO wastewater contains a high concentration of minerals that are pulled out of the tap water, so it will be too harsh for your plants.

Recap: Water

Plants use water to make food during photosynthesis.

Do not overwater plants!

The number one reason plants die is from being overwatered. If the roots are always wet, they will develop root rot.

Water plants when the soil is completely dry.

Stick your finger into the top layer of the soil. If it sticks, there is still water in the soil and you should not add more. If it is dry, wait a few days or a week to ensure all the soil is dry. Plants can survive dry spells longer than you might think.

If you overwatered your plant, move it into brighter light.

Bright light will help your plant use up water, and the excess water will evaporate from the soil. Just be careful not to leave some plants in hot light for too long, or the leaves will burn.

Water soil evenly and thoroughly.

When you water your plants, make sure that the water drains all the way through the soil and out of the bottom of the pot. Also, make sure to water all around the pot, not just one side.

Water the soil, not the leaves.

Only the roots absorb water. Extra water on the stem and leaves can lead to crown rot.

3

Soil

Soil is essential for most plants, but you'll notice that, unlike sunlight and water, it is not a direct part of photosynthesis. Instead, soil is almost like part of the plant, helping plants stand up, access water and break down nutrients in the soil, all of which help our plants grow. In many ways, soil is like your plant's stomach. Just as we have enzymes and microbes in our gut that help us digest food and process vitamins, soil contains microbes and nutrients that help your plants grow big and strong.

Soil helps maintain your plant's health in four ways:

- Regulates moisture
- Provides nutrition
- Maintains a healthy living ecosystem
- Provides support for the plant and its roots

Drainage: How soil regulates moisture

As we discussed in the chapter on water, if our plants receive too much water, they can rot and if our plants don't receive enough water, they can dry out and die. Of course, there's a wide spectrum when it comes to how much water different types of plant should receive, ranging from storage houses that live in dry conditions to plants like water lilies that live in standing water. Most plants that we take care of at home come from the forest or grasslands, so they fall somewhere in between.

When it rains, most of the water goes into the soil, where plants will then use their roots to seek out and absorb water to make energy through photosynthesis. Plants that live in water or in extremely dry areas have their own methods of regulating how much water they take in. But plants that live in the ground rely on the soil to help them regulate their water intake. For example, a wild bird of paradise plant may experience heavy rain after a long period of drought. Within a day, the bird of paradise plant will absorb as much water as it needs to make its food until the next big rain. The excess water will eventually sink deeper into the soil or be evaporated by the sun. As we can see, soil has the ability to hold water *and* drain water slowly over time.

Not all soils hold and drain water the same way, though. Loose soil made of large particles will drain water faster, whereas fine soil will hold water for a longer period. Tight and compact soil, like clay, may not even soak up water at all.

In nature, each plant has evolved to survive in a particular type of soil. Storage houses tend to live in sand, which drains water very fast; wanderers develop aerial roots to compensate for how far they extend away from the soil. It helps to know what kind of soil plants have in their natural environment because that kind of soil will also help them regulate water in a pot.

Living ecosystem: How soil breaks down nutrients for your plants

I think the most fascinating thing about soil is all the life it contains. Many of us walk around and think of all the living things that exist above ground, and if you've ever been snorkelling, you may consider all the life in our lakes, rivers and oceans. Most of the time, we think of soil as lifeless and desolate. But the truth is there are many living things in the soil, from insects and worms to bacteria and fungi. All these microorganisms play a role when it comes to the health of your plant because they form a community around its roots.

Not every living thing in the soil is going to help your plants. We know that certain bugs and fungi can kill them. But at the same time, there are many organisms that enrich the soil and break down nutrients for our plants. It is similar to how we have microorganisms in our bodies like probiotics that help us digest food, and antibodies that help us fight diseases. Just as not all microorganisms help us, not all microorganisms help our plants. We need to be careful about what we allow in our soil, and what we avoid, just as we are careful about what we eat or the medications we take.

Support: Soil keeps our plants standing upright

You may have observed that soil keeps our plants stable and balanced. But roots anchor plants in the soil, and different plants have different root systems. Different types of roots will affect how well a plant stands up in different types of soil as well as whether or not it will need any additional support. We can typically think about a plant's native environment to determine how long the roots will become and the type of soil that will support them best.

For example, cacti and other plants from desert areas have long roots because the water is often deep underground. These plants can get all the support they need in sand because their roots do most of the work. If we compare cacti to string of pearls or money plants, though, we find that the latter's root systems don't extend as deep underground. In nature, these plants benefit from a very nutritious and damp top layer of soil, so their roots don't need to go down very deep. Even then, wanderers such as money plants and tomato plants can benefit from a moss stick or a trellis that they can cling to for support, similar to the kind of support a nearby tree might provide in nature. If we want plants with shallow roots to grow larger leaves or bear more fruit, we must give them extra support.

The three major types of soil

Now that we understand the roles that soil plays for our plants, you may be thinking, 'How do I find out which type of soil provides the best drainage, nutrition, ecosystem and support for my plants?' Generally, there are three major categories of soil to consider based on their coarseness (or particle size): sand, clay and loam. The coarseness of each type of soil will affect both drainage and the amount of support it gives your plants.

Types of soil

Type of soil	Particle size	Drainage	Support
Sand	Large particles	Fast drainage	Minimal
Clay	Fine particles	Slow (or no drainage if it is very compressed)	Maximum
Loam	Mixture of fine and large particles	Moderate	Moderate

Why is drainage important? As I've mentioned before and cannot mention enough, we want to avoid root rot. The better the drainage, the less standing water we have. Some plants like standing water, but they are rare.

If you've ever been to the beach or played with sand, then you know it is a coarse type of soil. Sand is made of crushed shells and rocks, so it doesn't have a lot of nutrition, and it drains very fast.

Clay, on the other hand, is made of fine particles that are packed tightly together. Clay soil is formed when sediment deposits from rocks are put under pressure or go through prolonged moisture and dry spells, which is why we often find clay deep underground or in canyons.

Since clay offers very little room for air and water to move, or for roots to grow, should we avoid it altogether? Not necessarily. Some plants like clay and choosing the right soil for your plants is always a matchmaking process. While clay can be difficult to work with since it often needs to be broken up, there are many plants that grow well in clay soil such as castor bean, iris, shrubs and other stiff and sterns. Typically, these plants have a tough exterior that allows them to naturally break through the clay, but gardeners can also break up the clay to be more suitable for their plants.

Loam is often the first thing most people think of when they imagine the ideal soil. It is usually black or dark brown, and contains many different-sized particles, including wood chips, dirt, debris, silt and decayed matter. In nature, we find loam in forests, jungles and fields where there is a lot of organic matter that gets broken down over time by heat, rain, fungi, worms and insects. Loam is often rich in nutrients and can retain water fairly well while also providing a good amount of drainage. A large majority of plants do well in loamy soil, especially if they naturally grow in a forest and have a shallow root system or aerial roots.

How to choose the best soil for your plants?

One of the easiest ways to determine the right soil consistency for your plants (besides looking it up online) is to simply observe your plants and ask yourself:

- Does my plant store water?
- How deep is its root system?
- What environment would this plant grow well in if it was in nature?

If your plant has thick leaves or a rhizomal root structure, then it probably stores water and would do well in sand or clay soil. Plants that store water typically come from an area where the soil is dry, so we want to put them in a pot with soil that won't retain a lot of moisture.

On the other hand, if your plant has thin leaves, green stems, or aerial roots, then you probably want to put the plant in a loamy soil that will retain plenty of moisture. Wanderers and blooming wonders tend to love loamy soil, as well as many stiff and sterns and some storage houses.

If a plant is unfamiliar to you, do some research! I've looked up plenty of plants to learn where they are from and what soil would work best for them. Unlike light conditions, I recommend that you *do not* choose a soil type for your plant based on what kind of soil your plant had while at the nursery. Many nurseries use clay soil so that they can lift and move many plants at once, even though clay is not the best soil for the plant.

It's also worth noting that there are not many soils that check all the boxes when it comes to drainage, nutrition, ecosystem and support. You might need to add extra nutrients to make up for a lack of nutrition, or you may need to add a material like pumice stone to improve the drainage and aeration of the soil.

What about soil with coco peat as a base?

When you are shopping for soil, you will find there are some soils that use coco peat as a base. Coco peat (also called coco coir) is made from the coarse hairs found on coconut shells. Coco peat is a good soil base because it is a sterile material, meaning that it is less likely than other organic products to carry pathogens and diseases. Coco peat can retain moisture so that your plants are not sitting in water, but at the same time, there is still water available for your plant's roots. You don't have to water coco peat soil as frequently as you water other soils. Coco peat-based soil is good to use for plants that would normally prefer a loamy soil.

It is also possible to add coco peat to the soil you already have if you notice that it drains too fast, and you want your pot to retain more moisture. Coco peat is sold by itself in compacted bricks that gardeners can break up and mix into their soil.

Be thorough in your research when you are shopping for coco peat. Not all coco peat is equal. Start by making sure it looks right and is made up of coconut fibres, and that it doesn't have plastic or other stray items in it. When coco peat is made, small debris should be sieved out before it gets to you. If you see these items in your coco peat, it may be of low quality.

Another thing to check is the coco peat's electrical conductivity (EC). When you use coco peat as a base, it comes with a certain amount of electrical conductivity. If the conductivity is too high, it is bad for the plant. Ideally, one should choose coco peat with EC less than 0.8. If you actively use coco peat for gardening, you can check the conductivity with a tool called an EC meter. They are affordable and will keep you away from bad coco peat.

Pumice stone versus perlite for aeration and drainage

Pumice and perlite are two types of coarse material we can add to potting soil to improve aeration and drainage. Sometimes potting soil will include one of these materials already mixed into the soil. Both pumice and perlite originate from magma or lava, but they are slightly different.

Pumice stone is formed when lava and water mix together, and is usually a very rough and porous type of rock. Pumice stone is crushed into little bits that can be added to the soil, clearing space for air and water.

Perlite is made from volcanic glass that has been heated and expanded, and it usually looks like white flakes. Perlite is a much lighter material than pumice stone, so while it helps with aeration, I typically find that after a thorough watering, a lot of the perlite bits rise to the top of the soil, which doesn't help with drainage.

In my opinion, pumice stone is better than perlite; as it is heavier, it doesn't rise to the surface of the soil, so it is better for drainage. I recommend mixing pumice stone into the soil if you feel it is too hard or clumpy, or if water tends to sit on top of the soil and has a difficult time passing all the way through the drainage holes of your pot.

Complete soil versus additives

There are some nurseries and companies (such as the Lazy Gardener) who make 'complete soil' that includes nutrients, microbial activity and added materials for drainage and support. But most of the time, you will find that your soil is missing one or more of these components.

It is okay to purchase 'incomplete' soil but remember to add whatever is missing. For instance, if you purchase a coco peat-based loamy soil to repot your money plant but find that there aren't many nutrients in it, then you may want to purchase some slow-release fertilizer to mix into the soil. I would probably create a half-and-half mix to give my money plant plenty of extra nutrients so that it can make giant leaves!

You can usually read the bag or the description online to learn what the soil already includes and determine what may be missing. If you buy your soil from a nursery, then it is probably sold loose, in a clear bag with no description written on it. Most nursery soil is just the base soil with manure added for nutrition, in which case you may want to add pumice stone and microbes. You can always talk to the people at the nursery and learn what is in their soil.

When to give your plants new soil?

Unless your soil becomes infested by pests, you will never have to fully replace it. Instead, it is better to add any missing components and occasionally mix in a little fresh soil. For instance, if you notice that your plant has stopped growing, you may want to add nutrients and microbial fungi to kick off a new phase of growth.

A good time to add new soil, nutrients and microbes is when you are moving your plant to a new pot. Even if you bought a plant that the nursery kept in a pot of clay soil, it is okay to mix some of the clay into the new soil and fertilizer when you repot your plant.

The reason why we have to replace the soil if it becomes infested by pests is because there is no other effective way to control them. If your pot becomes infested with aphids or white flies, one of the only ways to rid your plant of the pests and their eggs is by repotting it into completely new, pest-free soil.

I typically like to freshen up the soil of a lot of plants at the same time. Repotting and tilling all my plants usually takes me four or five hours, but I like to make an afternoon out of it so that I have one giant mess to clean rather than a small mess every time I need to repot a plant.

Soil to drainage material ratio

When we are setting up our pots, we want to make sure to put a layer of coarse material at the bottom of the pot before adding soil to allow water to drain and provide extra support for our plants. I recommend using gravel as the bottom layer, but even in the soil itself, it is a good idea to mix in gravel or pumice stone to allow for general air flow, and to have organic matter in your pot that can be broken up by microbial activity over time.

Nutritious soil: The secret to larger and happier plants

I want to stress that good soil is worth the investment. I know, I know. You already bought a plant and the pot. Why spend extra money on something that comes from the ground?

But as we discovered, there is a lot more to soil than just dirt. Good soil is delicately balanced to do many things for our plants. Our plants aren't even aware of the pot. The pot might make us happy, but the soil is what makes our plants happy. It is their home, their source of nutrients, and the thing that keeps them rooted and grounded. These are our plant babies! We do not want to skimp on their home and their source of vitamins.

Many plants never get to experience their full potential. We might buy a plant, and it grows to a certain size, then stops growing. We water it and keep it alive, but we stop seeing changes in the size of our plants, and we stop seeing new growth.

Typically, our plants stop growing because we are not giving them enough nutrients. Just like we need calcium for our bones and an array of vitamins to help our hair, muscles and organs, our plants need nutrients to grow healthy roots, strong stems and beautiful leaves and flowers. So if you want your plant babies to grow up big and strong, you have to give them good, balanced, nutritious soil, starting when they're young.

Good soil saves plants. Problems like fungal infections, bacterial infections and overwatering will be easier to avoid if you start with the right kind of soil. If you buy a plant and it dies, you now have an empty pot and nothing to take care of. The money and time you spent on that plant was just a learning experience, which is fine if you apply what you learnt to your next plant. But now you are spending extra money for a second plant, which might also die if you don't give it the soil it needs to grow and thrive. Your plant is only ever going to be as good as its root system, so if we use a better soil to begin with, we now have a plant that keeps on growing, and we have made the most of our experience.

Try not to just buy the most expensive soil assuming it is the best. Do some research, think about what your plant needs and then shop accordingly. This could mean finding the best complete soil, or it could mean purchasing an okay base soil and adding in all the missing components.

We will talk more about nutrients and how to customize the right diet for your plant babies in the next section.

Recap: Soil

Soil helps plants regulate moisture, access nutrition, maintain a healthy living ecosystem and support itself and its roots.

There are generally three types of soil: sand, clay and loam.

Sand is made of large particles. Clay is made of fine particles that stick together. And loam is made from a mix of small and large particles.

Soil made of large particles drains water faster, while soil made of smaller particles absorbs and retains more water.

When deciding which soil is best for your plants, consider the support it needs and how well it can store water.

Plants that have thick roots and can store water can survive in sand, while plants that like ongoing access to water prefer loam. Be sure to add drainage material, such as gravel or pumice stone, to the bottom of your pots to help drain water.

Unless your soil becomes infested with pests, you shouldn't have to fully replace the soil in a pot.

It is better to add new soil and nutrients as the soil becomes compacted or when moving a plant to a larger pot.

Good soil is worth the investment.

For your plants to grow to their full potential, it is important to provide them with nutritious soil.

4

Nutrition

So far we have focused on how roots absorb water. But roots also absorb nutrients that serve many purposes, from blooming beautiful flowers to growing longer, stronger roots. You might have noticed that nutrients don't play a role in photosynthesis. This is because they are not used to create energy. Instead, nutrients are used to make new parts of the plant.

The difference between the energy that plants get from photosynthesis and the nutrients that plants absorb from the soil is similar to the difference between the calories and the nutrients in the food we eat. When you look at the nutritional information of a food, you will notice that it tells you how many calories are in the food as well as what vitamins it contains. The calories measure how much energy is in the food, while the nutrients and vitamins tell us how the food will help our bodies.

I love oranges. An orange has about sixty calories, which gives us about 3 per cent of our daily energy requirement. An orange also has about three grams of fibre, one gram of protein, fourteen micrograms of vitamin A and seventy milligrams of vitamin C. Fibre helps our digestive system. Protein helps repair cells and body tissue. Vitamin C boosts our immune system. And vitamin A sharpens our vision and boosts our immunity. I remember when I was younger, my dad would always encourage us to eat plenty of papaya, not because we weren't getting enough energy but because he wanted Keerti and I to get plenty of vitamin A. Now that I'm a proud plant dad, I have to make sure my plants get all their vitamins and nutrients too.

The three major nutrients for plants are nitrogen, phosphorus and potassium. Plants use nitrogen to make protein. Most plant tissue, including the stems, stalks and leaves, is formed from proteins that utilize nitrogen. Phosphorus helps plants use and store energy, especially when they are growing roots and flowers. And potassium strengthens the leaves and roots so that they can fight off diseases and survive cold temperatures.

In addition to these three major nutrients, there are thousands of micronutrients in the soil that plants use to grow big, strong and healthy.

Slow-release versus quick-release nutrients

When we think about what kind of nutrients our plants need, it is important to consider how old our plants are. Are they still babies? Teenagers? Or mature plants?

The age of your plants will determine whether they need slow-release or quick-release nutrients. Some nutrients such as ammonium and nitrates can be used by your plant almost as soon as they are put into the soil. Other slow-release nutrients come from compounds that either need to be broken down by microbes or must dissolve slowly in water before the plant can use them.

Younger plants, especially starting as a seed or a sapling, benefit more from quick-release nutrients. Your seed or baby plant needs access to nutrients as soon as possible so that it can get the energy and materials it needs to break through the soil and unfurl its roots and stem. Big plants, or plants that we are repotting, benefit from slow-release nutrients; they already have long roots to drink water and big leaves to take in the sun. Now, all they need is some long-term access to nutrients that will help them become more efficient at making food through photosynthesis.

Remember, though, that microbial activity might be required to break down long-term nutrients into a form that the roots can ingest. If the soil or fertilizer doesn't already have certain types of microbes, you may need to add yogurt, compost or manure to the soil, which should help it break down nutrients.

NPK: The macronutrients nitrogen, phosphorus and potassium

Just like people need carbohydrates, protein and fats, plants need nitrogen, phosphorus and potassium. Botanists and biologists often refer to these three nutrients as 'macronutrients', meaning that plants should have an abundance of each of these three elements. Bags of fertilizer list 'NPK' on the front of the bag with the ratio of each. These are the chemical symbols for each nutrient, with 'N' being nitrogen, 'P' being phosphorus and 'K' being potassium.

Importance of nutrients

Nutrient	What it does for our plants	How it naturally gets into the soil	When to give to your plant
Nitrogen (N)	Major component in chlorophyll and plant proteins. Helps your plants grow big, strong, healthy leaves	Comes from organic matter that has been decomposed by microorganisms	Should always be present in soil. Best to add year-round
Phosphorus (P)	Found in every plant cell. Helps with energy transfer, photosynthesis, nutrient movement, transformation of sugar and starches, and the passing along of genetic characteristics in propagation and plant reproduction	Natural component of minerals found in the ground	Springtime, or before your plant's blooming season
Potassium (K)	Activates enzymes that help plants use water, resist drought, grow flowers and regulate photosynthesis	Contained in minerals, sometimes coming from the decomposition of organic matter like mushrooms and bananas	Springtime, or before your plant's blooming season

As you can see, nitrogen helps with general plant growth while phosphorus and potassium work together to transfer energy and regulate photosynthesis. It's especially important to give your blooming wonders extra potassium to help them grow flowers. Nitrogen, phosphorus and potassium are the three *main* nutrients that plants need, but there are hundreds of micronutrients that also help our plants.

Micronutrients

If nitrogen, phosphorus and potassium are to plants as carbohydrates, fats and protein are to humans, then micronutrients are similar to our vitamins. Most fertilizer brands include a balance of macronutrients, but I find that what is often overlooked by gardeners is the importance of micronutrients. The term 'micronutrients' indicates that plants need less of these nutrients than they do of the macronutrients, but they are still vital to the health of our plants.

While there are many different micronutrients for plants, there are eight that are important to include in any soil:

- Zinc
- Manganese
- Magnesium
- Molybdenum
- Iron
- Boron
- Copper
- Calcium

Each of these micronutrients helps in the development of different parts of the plant. For instance, zinc is an important component of chlorophyll, while iron is used by plants for pigmentation and energy production. Molybdenum helps plants absorb phosphorus, so even if you include a fertilizer with NPK, it won't make the most use of phosphorus if you do not also include molybdenum. Some fertilizers and 'complete' soils will include all, or some, of the eight micronutrients listed above.

Another way to add micronutrients to soil is by adding seaweed extract. Seaweed extract is a great broad-spectrum source of micronutrients for plants. I think of it like a multivitamin that includes a small dose of all the vitamins we should have for a healthy body. Seaweed is packed with nutrients because it is a complex colony of algae and plankton that attracts a wide range of nutrients and microorganisms as it grows. Because seaweed includes so many nutrients, it is the primary food source for most fish and is popular in many cuisines and supplements for humans, too.

There are thousands of different types of seaweed that range in colour, size, shape and structure. Seaweed fertilizers are classified by the types of algae found in the seaweed, and they come in granules, liquids, concentrates, powders and foliar sprays. I typically recommend seaweed fertilizers that contain the algae ascophyllum.

While seaweed extract is a good way to introduce a lot of different types of micronutrients to the soil's ecosystem, there are times when you may want to add a specific nutrient that is lacking. Similar to when our body is deficient in one vitamin, it is better to take that single vitamin rather than a multivitamin. If you are deficient in vitamin C, it would be better to take a vitamin C pill or eat an orange, rather than take a multivitamin that includes only a small amount of vitamin C.

How do nutrients get inside our plants? Our bodies break down vitamins, but plants do not have digestive systems like we do. Instead, the soil does the work of breaking down the nutrients before the plants can use them. For instance, phosphorus cannot be absorbed by the roots until a microbial fungi breaks it down into orthophosphorus.

Let us take a closer look at the fascinating world of life below the surface and learn how it helps (or hurts) our plants.

It's alive! Meet the organisms that live in soil

Think about dirt. What comes to mind?

When most people look at a patch of dirt, they see a cold, lifeless place where everything decays. But there is an entire web of life underground. I'm not talking about mole men or people living in bunkers; I'm referring to all the microscopic organisms such as fungi, bacteria and worms that spend their lives moving about, reproducing, eating things and leaving by-products in the soil.

Fungi

Fungi are some of the most varied forms of life that we find in and above the soil. Fungi come in many shapes and sizes, ranging from large, colourful mushrooms to tiny microorganisms. Fungi are different from plants and animals in that they reproduce using spores and they feed off organic matter.

Unlike plants, fungi cannot make their own food, but in the process of breaking down organic matter, they can help plants access nutrients. On the other hand, some fungi feed on the plants themselves. So there are both fungi that can help our plants grow, and fungi that can kill our plants.

Let's look at some of the heroic fungi that safeguard plants as well as the villainous fungi that endanger them.

Good fungi that break down nutrients and help our plants

I find that many people associate fungi with disease and poor hygiene. We learn to throw out food with mould on it, and wash between our toes to prevent athlete's foot. But some fungi can help us. Penicillin, which is derived from fungi, is used by doctors to treat bacterial infections. Much like some fungi can help us humans, certain fungi can help plants access nutrients, fight off infections and grow longer, healthier root systems.

Mycorrhizal fungi: A partnership rooted in growth

Mycorrhizal fungi have a symbiotic relationship with plants, meaning that the plant takes care of the fungus, and the fungus takes care of the plant. There are two main types of mycorrhizal fungi: ectomycorrhizal fungi, which live near a plant's root system, and endomycorrhizal fungi, which live *inside* a plant's roots. Both types receive sugar from the plant, and in turn help the plant's roots grow longer to access extra water and transfer phosphorus. Some types of endomycorrhizal fungi expand the cell membranes within the roots to reach deeper within the soil, which is how we get those long root systems with secondary and tertiary roots.

Mycorrhizal fungi

Mycorrhizal fungi should already be abundant in most soils, but through the process of watering and tilling (upturning the soil), you may find that your soil is lacking in mycorrhizal fungi. This is especially true for plants in pots where the soil is separated from rest of the ecosystem and there is no way for natural replenishment. When soil lack mycorrhizal fungi you would find the plant to have very few tertiary roots. It is easiest to observe when repotting the plants.

Trichoderma: A bodyguard for roots

Trichoderma is another type of fungi that helps plants fight off fungal infections. Trichoderma, like endomycorrhizal fungi, grows on the roots of plants, forming a barrier between the roots and other fungi that can cause disease and infection. Trichoderma is an amazing fungus because it allows good pathogens, nutrients and fungi to enter the plant's root system while defending against bad fungi that can cause root rot and blight. In fact, Trichoderma is parasitic to most bad fungi, meaning that it can destroy bad fungi found in the soil around the roots before they can attack the plant.

Trichoderma is naturally found in most soils. But since we buy soil that has been sitting in a bag, most Trichoderma remains dormant. I usually recommend gardeners add Trichoderma to their soil when first potting their plant because it is a great way to prevent root rot and other infections and diseases.

Note: Trichoderma only works *before* there is an infection. If bad fungi have already attacked your plant, Trichoderma can't help it.

Mushrooms: Your friendly neighbourhood fungi

Although they are not commonly found in houseplant soil, you may occasionally notice mushrooms pop up in your pot, especially if you keep your plants in a humid environment. Most mushrooms will not harm your plant. They break up the soil, making it easier for your plants to access nutrients. You do not have to remove mushrooms, but you may want to if you have pets or small children who may try to eat them.

Sometimes mushrooms can be tricky to remove if they have already laid down spores in the soil. If you notice only one mushroom, simply remove it from the base, being careful not to shake off any spores that can grow new mushrooms. You may also want to dig out the top layer of soil around the area where the mushroom was growing and add new soil. If mushrooms keep appearing around your plant, you may need to repot it. But once again, if you are not worried about your pets or children eating the mushrooms, it is usually better to just leave them.

Bad fungi

While fungi like mycorrhizae and Trichoderma protect our plants and help them grow, some other fungi eat away at our plants, causing them to decay and die.

Sooty mould: The black plague of plants

Sooty mould is a black fungus that grows on top of leaves. Sooty mould doesn't feed off plants. Instead, it feeds off the honeydew secretions left behind by pests such as aphids and flies. Sooty mould harms plants by blocking the pores on the leaf and preventing them from absorbing sunlight. If you have sooty mould on your plant, first clean the leaves with a damp cloth. Be careful not to shake the fungus spores back on to the plant or soil.

While sooty mould can travel in the air, it is most often caused when pests have taken a liking to your plant. So after cleaning your plant's leaves, you may want to move your plant or spray the leaves and soil with neem or another non-toxic pesticide.

Powdery mildew: Dreadful dust

Powdery mildew is another fungus that often starts on the leaves but can spread to the entire plant, making it weak and frail. As the name suggests, powdery mildew looks like a fine white powder that coats the leaves of your plants. If you notice powdery mildew on your plant's leaves, first prune off all the leaves with the mildew on them. Once again, be careful not to shake the spores from the infected leaves on to the other leaves or the soil. Once you have removed all the infected leaves, you may want to move your plant to a brighter area, or to a place where it can get more air circulation. Powdery mildew thrives in dim light and stale air. Be sure to wash your hands with soap and water after handling your plant, and regularly wipe its leaves with a damp cloth to prevent the mildew from coming back.

Grey mould: Withers away plants in winter

Grey mould usually shows up as tan or grey spores on the base, stem and leaves of the plant. Grey mould grows in cold, humid conditions and typically infects weak spots such as broken stems, where it will cause the plant to shrivel and collapse. Grey mould should be taken care of as soon as you notice it, since it can quickly spread throughout your plant. I recommend that you wear gloves and carefully remove all infected areas. Take your bypass shears and cut off any infected leaves, stems and branches. Remember to wash your tools between each cut so that you do not spread more spores around the plant. Also, be careful not to breathe in the mould spores; you may want to wear a face mask.

Once you have removed all the infected areas, your plant may look a little sad. As long as the mould has not spread to the root system, it has a chance of surviving. You may want to apply a fungicide to kill any mould in the soil that you might have missed. Fungicide could kill the good fungi as well, so you can add some Trichoderma to the soil after a few weeks and a good watering. You should also move your plant to a warmer area with less humidity so that it doesn't attract more grey mould.

Pythium, phytophthora and rhizoctonia: The culprits of rot

Pythium, phytophthora and rhizoctonia are the three types of fungi that can cause root rot, stem rot and crown rot. Typically, by the time you notice these fungal infections, it is very difficult to save your plant.

If the rotted areas are only above the soil, you may be able to remove all infected parts of the plant and nurse the root system back to health. But if the roots are infected, your only chance is to take an uninfected cutting and attempt to propagate a new plant.

When it comes to fungal rot, prevention is the best cure. Pythium, phytophthora and rhizoctonia are all attracted to moist, cool environments, which is why I always emphasize good drainage and having the right light for your plants. If your pot can drain water, there is less of a chance that it will stay moist for a long period of time and attract these kinds of fungi. In addition to having a good drainage system, I also recommend that you mix Trichoderma into the soil.

Remember: Trichoderma is the protector of plants. It will fight off and destroy the evil fungi before they have a chance to attack your plant babies.

Bacteria

Bacteria are another wide-ranging type of life form that can be found in soil—if you look at it under a microscope. Bacteria are often single-celled organisms, so they cannot always be seen by the naked eye. Just like fungi, there are good bacteria that help our plants and bad bacteria that can hurt them.

Probiotics: Your plant's digestive buddy

A type of good bacteria that you are probably already familiar with is probiotic bacteria. As you may know, probiotics are found in food like yogurt and fermented vegetables, and they keep our digestive system healthy by fighting off germs and breaking down food. Probiotics serve a similar function for plants, breaking down compounds in the soil into nutrients that roots can absorb. There are many ways to add probiotics to soil, including taking a scoop of curd or yogurt and mixing it in. But I find the best way to cultivate probiotics is by creating my own compost at home.

Bacterial disease in plants

While bacterial diseases are rarer than fungal infections, sometimes your plants can become infected with strains of airborne or waterborne bacteria. Bacterial infections typically start on an open wound on your plant, like a leaf or stem that has been cut poorly. I always recommend using sharp shears when pruning to make a clean cut that our plants can naturally form a callus around within a few hours. When we use blunt tools or tear at our plants, we often leave big scars that are difficult to heal, leaving them exposed to bacteria in the air.

Another way to prevent bacterial infections is by always giving plants clean, filtered water. Some bacteria can be found in water, but we can remove it before it gets to our plants by using water that has been filtered in some way, including fresh rainwater, carbon-filtered water or AC drain water.

Worms

Earthworms are the most common type of worms we find in potting soil because they are used to make vermicompost. Most earthworms are removed from compost before it is bagged and sold in stores, but sometimes the earthworm eggs will stay in the soil and hatch in our pots. Many gardeners consider earthworms to be friendly helpers that aerate the soil, and for the most part, I agree. If you find an earthworm in your soil, it is okay to let it stay. The worm will move about, creating new passageways for air, and will digest organic matter, unlocking more nutrients for your plant.

However, not all worms are friendly. Hookworms, tapeworms and roundworms all live underground, and can be parasitic to humans and animals and make us sick if they find their way into our digestive system. Most soil brands have a process for removing these kinds of worms, as do farmers before sending vegetables to the store. But some parasitic worms can still make their way into gardening soil. Whenever you handle potting soil, take precautions: wear gardening gloves, wash your hands after touching soil and avoid touching your face. Do not let your pets or children ingest the soil.

Recap: Nutrients

Plants use nutrients to grow big, healthy and strong.

Slow-release nutrients versus quick-release nutrients.

Younger plants need faster access to nutrients, so it is better to use quick-release nutrients on baby plants, and slow-release nutrients on mature plants.

The three major nutrients for plants are nitrogen, phosphorus and potassium (NPK).

Nitrogen is a major component of chlorophyll and plant proteins. Phosphorous helps plants transfer energy in their cells. Potassium activates enzymes that help plants use water and grow flowers.

There are also thousands of micronutrients that plants use to become and stay healthy.

Many micronutrients help plants absorb the macronutrients. One way to add micronutrients to soil is by adding seaweed extract.

Microorganisms in the soil help break down nutrients for your plant.

Microorganisms include fungi, bacteria and some worms. There are both good and bad microorganisms. We want to add good microorganisms to the soil to help break down micronutrients.

Part III

Ongoing Care for Your Plant

We've learnt the basics of plant care, but how do we make it a habit? Our plant babies may be easier to care for than a real baby or a pet dog or cat, but they're also easier to forget about. Plants don't cry or beg for food when they're hungry. Most of the time when someone says 'I kill every plant' or 'I don't have a green thumb', it's simply because they forgot about the plant after a couple of weeks.

I will admit that new habits can be hard to form. Without awareness, it's easy to forget that you're trying to add a new practice into your life. You have a plant now, but you still get up, make breakfast, brush your teeth, go to work and then on your way to work you might remember, 'Oh! I forgot to check on my new plant!'

The best way to adopt a new habit is to be patient, intentional and consistent. For the first few weeks, you may want to set a reminder on your phone or leave a sticky note on your mirror that says, 'Check on plants'. After a few weeks or a month of reminding yourself, checking on your plants should become as natural as brushing your teeth.

Taking care of plants every day is what makes someone a gardener. Especially when we care for plants in our home, we need to be mindful because we're in control of their environment.

In the wild, the climate and ecosystem will naturally provide for plants. There might be fluctuations in temperature, a storm or an infestation that kills many plants in nature, but there are also enough plants that the surviving plants will go on to reproduce and repopulate. Of course, climate change, fires and deforestation can wipe out forests, so we want to be mindful of the impact human activity has on our natural environment.

But in our homes, a plant depends entirely on us. Our plant babies may be durable, but you still have to give them light and water and tend to their needs. It is up to you to check the moisture in their soil, look out for pests and diseases, and ensure they grow. In addition, we need to trim them, till their soil, pay attention to their leaves and repot them when needed.

Ongoing care also includes growing as a gardener by propagating new plant babies, building a community around gardening and spreading the joy of plants both in your society and around the world.

1

Trimming and Pruning: Giving Your Plant a Haircut

If you want bushy plants, you have to trim them. The idea that a plant will grow more when you trim it surprises many plant parents, and it surprised me, too. It seems counterintuitive, right? How does making something smaller make it bigger?

I find that 'trim and it will grow more' is the most difficult piece of advice for gardeners to follow. A lot of plant parents are scared to cut their plants. If their plant has one big leaf and a single stem, they don't want to snip it. They might think, 'This is how my plant wants to grow, so I don't want to mess with it', or 'What if instead of a bushier plant, I lose the one leaf that has managed to grow?!'

My family faced a similar dilemma with a curry leaf plant that we had on our balcony. We wanted it to become bushier, with more branches and leaves, but we were reluctant to trim it. Curry leaf plants have to be trimmed back from the main stem, which means losing all the leaves. For weeks, my mother wouldn't let us cut it. But we decided that since we had multiple curry leaf plants, it was worth taking the risk and cutting the one stem. To our pleasant surprise, more branches and leaves started to grow. That plant is still alive and we still trim it, knowing that it will grow back.

Why do our plants grow when we prune them? When we cut our plants, their instinct kicks in and they feel that they are in danger. They feel threatened and think, 'I am under attack'. A plant hormone, auxin, found at the tip of branches prevents further branching of that specific branch. So when we remove the tip by pruning the auxin is removed and the branch cannot create new branches. This encourages the plant to grow laterally, create new branches and become bushier, as a way to survive.

In nature, plants get torn up all the time. An animal or insect may feed on them, take some foliage to build a nest, or simply run through a tangle of leaves and rip them up. When a plant grows, it produces a hormone called auxin at the tip of each stem or branch. Auxin prevents the plant from getting bushy. But when a stem or branch tip is cut or torn, the plant can grow more stems from that area because it stops producing that hormone. I imagine with our curry leaf plant, it thinks, 'My one long stem is under attack! Maybe I should grow more stems just in case.' Of course, we're not attacking it. We're helping it grow.

Most plants can be easily pruned. Just make sure not to cut away too much of the plant because it still needs to gather sunlight and photosynthesize for new growth.

When to trim and prune your plants

There are a few reasons why we want to trim our plants:

1) We want to encourage new growth and branching paths (especially before the growing season)
2) We notice that part of the plant has a disease or dead leaves
3) We want to change the shape of our plant

You can generally trim plants any time of the year, but it is especially important to trim your plants before spring and before the monsoon season. I like to trim my plants in late February or early March to encourage growth in the spring. And then I trim my plants again around July before the monsoon season starts. In India, springtime and the monsoon season are when our plants tend to grow the most, so it is best to prepare them for growth with a good trim.

Tools for pruning your plants

There are two main tools that we use to prune and trim our plants: bypass pruners and anvil pruners.

Bypass pruners and anvil shears

Bypass pruners are like regular scissors with a single-edged blade that slices *past* a thick base as it closes. Unlike normal scissors, a bypass pruner has a very sharp, curved blade that makes precise, clean, quick cuts to the stem. Bypass pruners are designed to be used to trim green stems on plants like pilea, money plants and most other wanderers and blooming wonders.

Anvil pruners have one sharp blade on top that closes on the centre of a flat surface, much like the flat surface of an anvil is used to forge and temper metal. Anvil pruners are like a knife and a cutting board: the blade does the cutting, and the flat board provides a surface to cut against. They are designed for stiff and sterns and other plants with brown, hard stems that have a wood-like texture, such as bougainvillea and hibiscus. Anvil pruners are also good for trimming off dead stems.

We always want to make sure that our pruners are sharp because we want the cuts to be clean. If we have to pull and tug at the plant to trim it, then we can damage the plant tissue, which can lead to infections and destroy the plant.

How to prune your plants

Trimming and pruning plants shouldn't be complicated. It is easy to become overwhelmed when first cutting your plant because you probably think, 'I don't want to hurt my baby!' But as we discussed, it is better for the plant and something that it would probably experience in nature. Just think of it like a haircut!

The first thing I ask myself when pruning is, 'Can this plant be propagated? Can I use it to make a new plant?' If it can, then I want to cut it at a place where I know roots will form so that I can grow the cutting in water or a new pot. Bumps on the stem (nodes) are typical places where new roots can emerge from.

Once I've looked carefully at my plant and decided where I want to trim, I select the right tool. As we learnt above, we should choose bypass pruners for green plants, and anvil pruners for stiff and sterns.

When I have the right tool, I get to cutting. If you're not sure where to cut, you can generally cut back a few centimetres from the tip of each branch or stem and be fine. I generally like to cut back to the part of the stem or branch where I still see happy leaves and find that where I cut, a split path will grow with more leaves. Many times, deciding where to cut is a matter of opinion, but we should always cut off parts of the plant that look infected or diseased.

We also want to trim blooming wonders when their flowers start to wilt, which is called 'deadheading'. It's fairly simple. Just grab your bypass shears and trim the stem just below the wilted flower.

The reason we deadhead is that we don't know which flowers have pollinated, and we don't want our plant to waste energy creating seeds. Trimming the flowers off when they wilt promotes more blooming and less seeds and keeps the flowering plant alive.

Recap: Trimming and pruning

If you want bushy plants, you have to trim them.

Another word for trimming is pruning.

Deadheading is another type of pruning when you snip off wilted flowers.

There are three reasons why we trim our plants:

1) To encourage new growth or branching paths
2) A part of the plant has a disease or dead leaves
3) We want to change the shape of our plant

It's especially important to trim your plants in the spring and before the monsoon season to encourage new growth.

There are two types of pruners: bypass pruners and anvil pruners.

Bypass pruners have two blades that pass each other; they are designed to trim soft stems. Anvil pruners have one sharp blade that closes on a flat surface; they are designed for plants with stiff, hard stems.

Trimming your plants shouldn't be complicated.

Use the right tool. Cut away any dead parts of the plant. If you want to propagate the cutting, be sure to include any areas you would need for propagation, such as aerial nodes.

2

Tilling the Soil

Tilling is one of the most overlooked ways to help plants. We focus a lot on watering, but for water and air to get to the roots, we need to till.

Tilling is when we use a flat tool to loosen and upturn the soil. Over time, due to gravity and watering, the soil will start to compact in the pot, which can close off air passages. Every two to three months, we want to till the soil to give the roots more air to breathe and give water more room to move through the soil.

I also like to till the soil whenever I add new fertilizer or microbes so that they can be evenly distributed around the roots. You can tell that the soil needs to be tilled if there is algae on the top layer or if water isn't draining out of the drainage holes. Algae is a sign that water is pooling on the top of the soil, which means the soil is too compact. If there is algae on the top of the soil, it is okay to till it and dig it back into the soil because algae contains nutrients that are good for our plants.

To till the soil, you can use a *khurpi*, trowel or any other blunt, thin tool. Our goal is to mix the soil above and near the roots without damaging them, which can be tricky. As we know, the roots are important.

The trick is to move slowly and use the right-sized tool; the smaller the pot, the smaller the khurpi. If you use a khurpi that is too big, you have a greater chance of accidentally damaging your plant.

Start from the edge and insert your khurpi about an inch into the soil. Take your time. If it is a deep pot, or you know your plant has deep roots, you may want to go down two or three inches. Continue to poke your khurpi straight down into the soil in different areas, moving around the pot, being careful not to get too close to the roots. We want to till fairly close to the roots, but not so close that we cut them. By going down into the soil and around the pot, you should be able to create new passageways for air and water to move through the soil.

Recap: Tilling the soil

Tilling is when we use a flat tool to loosen and upturn the soil.

It is good to till the soil every two to three months to give the roots more air to breathe and give water more room to move through the soil.

It is also good to till the soil whenever you add new fertilizer or microbes so they can be evenly distributed around the roots.

To till the soil, you can use a khurpi, trowel or any other blunt, thin tool.

Be careful not to damage the roots when you till!

3

What Your Plants' Leaves Are
Trying to Tell You

In addition to watering our plants, giving them nutrients, trimming them and moving them around to get the right light, we also need to be mindful of anything we can do to make them happier. When you check in with your plants every day, you will notice subtle changes in their mood and have a better understanding of when they need some love and attention.

Cleaning your plants' leaves

You may notice that your plant's leaves get dusty. Even inside a home or apartment, you will find that dust accumulates fairly quickly on the large, flat leaves of plants like monstera, money plant or pilea. About once a month, I notice a significant layer of dust on most of my plants' leaves. Dust blocks light and clogs the pores of the leaf, making it difficult for your plant to photosynthesize and respire. By removing the dust from each leaf, I find that the leaves grow faster and live longer, and the plant as a whole stays happy.

To wipe the dust off the leaf, I simply get a moist cloth, gently hold the leaf by the stem so that I don't accidentally pull it off, and run the cloth over the leaf from the base to the tip. I do this with all the leaves until there is no more dust. While most of the dust will gather on top of the leaves, some dust can also gather on the underside of the leaves, so remember to wipe both sides.

Wiping off every leaf with a cloth is the best method to clean the dust off a plant, but it can be tedious. If you are short on time and want to quickly remove some of the dust, you can also mist your plants' leaves with a spray bottle. The water will make some of the dust fall from the leaves. Avoid using the misting method for plants like succulents and spider plants that are susceptible to crown rot.

Troubleshooting leaves: Understanding yellow and brown leaves

Ah yes, the troublesome yellow leaf. Almost every gardener has the moment when they see a leaf turning yellow and their heart stops. 'What does it mean? Is my plant going to die?'

I have some good news. It is usually okay if your plant's leaves turn yellow. Even if a plant with yellow leaves is having issues, many of those issues can be easily resolved.

Leaves can turn yellow for a variety of reasons:

- The leaf is at the end of its life cycle
- Pests are attacking the plant

- Lack of sunlight
- Lack of nutrition
- Change in temperature
- Light is too bright
- Too much water
- Not enough water

If you see yellow leaves, try not to worry. Yellow leaves usually aren't a big deal, especially if the plant is a few years old and the leaves that are turning yellow are some of the original leaves on the plant. It's natural for leaves to age, turn yellow and fall off.

When leaves turn yellow because they have reached the end of their life cycle, you'll notice that it is a uniform yellow, starting from the stem. You typically will not have to cut or prune these leaves; they will shed on their own. Like leaves that change colour and fall from trees during the fall season, just a touch of your finger or a gust of wind will make them fall from your plant.

When should we worry about yellow leaves?

Of course, there are times when a leaf turns yellow and your plant *is* trying to tell you something. So how do we know if the leaf is yellow because it's old, or if our plant is trying to warn us?

If you notice one yellow leaf, it is probably not a big deal, and it is just reaching the end of its life cycle. But if you notice multiple yellow leaves, take a closer look at your plant and think about any recent changes to the plant's environment. Have you moved your plant? Has the temperature changed? Have you used a new fertilizer? Are you watering it differently? Is the drainage system of the pot clogged?

One of the first things I check for are signs of pests because they are typically the most visible cause of yellow leaves. Look at the stem. Are there any white spots that could be bugs? Push the soil around with your finger. Do you notice any mites or insects? If so, then your plant's leaves are turning yellow because the insects are eating your plant, in which case it is time to repot the plant in clean soil and clean any insects off the plant itself. If pests are the reason your plant's leaves are turning yellow, you will only notice one or a few yellow leaves.

If you notice many leaves turning yellow at once, it is probably a sign that your plant is missing something or has too much of something, whether that's light, nutrients or water. Remember that leaves are green because they have chlorophyll. Chlorophyll is made of magnesium, so if your plant is not getting enough magnesium, the leaves will lose some of their greenish hue.

If you notice the leaf starts yellowing at the tip, and only the top half of the leaf turns yellow while the bottom half remains its natural colour, it might not be getting enough light or the soil may be lacking in certain nutrients. The veins might still be green as well. When the veins of the plant are green and the yellow is radiating outwards, this is a clear sign that there is a lack of light or nutrients. If you see a yellow leaf with green veins, try moving the plant to a brighter area and feed your plant a fertilizer or plant food that is rich in magnesium such as Epsom salt.

Leaves can also change colour if your plant gets too cold. Typically, though, when plants are cold, their leaves turn a pale yellow or an almost white colour. Make sure that your plants stay at a stable temperature. If your plant has been in twenty degrees Celsius temperature its entire life, it will not be happy if the temperature drops more than five or ten degrees below that. If you keep your plants outside and they get cold, either move them inside or wrap their pot in a towel. You can even follow Indian tradition and place a chunni over your plant when it is cold; this will help it stay warm and retain heat. During the cold season, I typically move my plants inside so that I can regulate the temperature and they can stay happy and warm.

What about brown leaves?

Typically, leaves that turn brown will also be crispy and dry, indicating that either your plant is too hot or that it needs water. If you see a brown spot that looks more like a circle, it is most likely a burn, in which case you should move your plant away from any high-temperature sources of heat. Your plant's leaves can get burnt by both direct light that is too hot, or heat from a heater or a hot object like a stove, candle, hot light bulb or an outdoor AC unit.

If the leaves are brown and crispy starting from the tip, then it is most likely a sign that your plant is dehydrated and needs to be watered. Leaves that are dehydrated will also shrink in size. But be careful. Sometimes a brownish yellow leaf could mean that your plant has been *overwatered*.

Touch the leaf. Is it soft or crispy?

If it is soft, sticky, moist or spongy, your plant is receiving too much water. In that case, more water will *hurt* your plant. Move your plant to a brighter area and make sure that the drain holes on the bottom of the pot are not clogged. You may also want to repot your plant, which we will cover in the next section.

If the leaf is brown and crispy and the soil is bone-dry, water the soil. Review the watering section for more details about when and how to water your plant.

What to do if your plant has yellow or brown leaves?

What should we do when our plants have yellow leaves?

I recommend that we don't do anything but remove the yellow leaves and then wait about five days. Plants take their time to adjust, so we don't want to be too reactive and expect quick fixes. The yellow leaves may be a sign of a problem that occurred a few weeks ago.

Of course, if your plant is too close to a heat source, move it.

If you can see that there are pests attacking the plant, get rid of the pests.

Otherwise give it time to adjust. If the yellow leaves return the following week, then you know that there is probably a bigger problem that needs to be fixed.

Also check to see if there is new growth. Sometimes if a plant is unhappy above the soil because it is too cold or because it is losing old leaves, it will grow new stems from the soil. If the old part of your plant looks like it is dying but there is new growth coming out of the soil, then your plant is still alive and happy. Your plant is simply reaching the end of one cycle and starting a new cycle of life and growth. I've brought many plants back to life that looked like they were dead on top. The key is to be patient, look for signs of new growth and water the soil whenever it is completely dry.

Recap: What your plants' leaves are trying to tell you

When you check on your plants, you may notice subtle changes in their leaves.

If you notice that the leaves are dusty, wipe the dust off with a moist cloth or damp towel.

Leaves can turn yellow for a variety of reasons:

- The leaf is at the end of its life cycle
- Pests are attacking the plant
- Lack of sunlight
- Lack of nutrition
- Change in temperature
- Light is too bright
- Too much water
- Not enough water

Be patient. Make small adjustments when addressing brown or yellow leaves.

When leaves are brown and crispy it usually means your plant is too hot or needs water.

A sticky brownish-yellow leaf may mean you're overwatering. Move it to bright sunlight.

Check for new growth. If a plant has yellow leaves but also has new growth, the yellow leaves have probably just reached the end of their life cycle.

4

Repotting Your Plant

Plants can stay in the same pot for a long time, and all we have to do is occasionally give them water and replenish their nutrients. But there are a few instances, some of which we already discussed, where your plant will be happier in a new pot:

- Your plant has outgrown its pot
- Pests have infested the soil
- Your plant is in a pot that is too big
- The roots are infected

When we see the roots coming out of the bottom of the pot or poking out of the top of the soil, this means that there is less soil in the pot and more roots. In other words, it is root-bound. When we water these root-bound plants, there is very little soil to hold the water, and there are a lot of roots to quickly absorb the water. Eventually, what you will find is that the plant tends to dry out fast and you may see those brown, crispy leaves that mean your plant is dehydrated because it needs more water than you can give it in a single watering. If you notice that your plant is root-bound and soaks up all the water you give it within a day, it is probably time to move your plant into a larger pot.

Signs that your plant has outgrown its pot:

- Roots coming out of the top of the soil
- Roots growing out of the drainage holes
- You hit roots at the surface when you till the soil
- Your plant has brown, crispy leaves despite regular watering

Typically, plants can survive being root-bound, but they won't grow any bigger. Wanderers like syngonium, Wandering Jew and money plants like to be root-bound in the pot because they can grow roots along the stem and still get the extra water and nutrition they need to grow. As long as we encourage their nodes to grow roots with a moss stick or wet paper towels, these wanderers will continue to wander and grow. But for most plants, we probably want to repot them a few weeks after we

Root-bound plants

notice that their roots have begun to outgrow the pot that they are in.

Finding the right pot for your plant

Whether you're buying a pot for a new plant or you're looking for a pot to repot your plant, it's easy to get overwhelmed by all the options. How big should it be? What colour? Should it be plastic or ceramic? Metal or terracotta?

Pots serve three purposes:

- Pots are decorative
- Pots provide a drainage system for our plants
- Pots hold the soil and the plant, allowing the plant to stay contained while also allowing it to get fresh air

Whether or not you like how a certain pot looks is a matter of opinion, just like your personal style. I admit that it is nice to find a pot that matches my plant or looks good on the shelf. But how the pot looks in terms of colour and pattern doesn't affect how well the plant will survive and grow.

What is essential, though, is how well the pot will drain water, and whether or not the pot will give the plant room to breathe and grow. Often, we are looking for a pot that is slightly larger than the previous pot so that our plant has more room to grow. Nurseries measure pot size by diameter, so a six-inch pot means that the space across the top of the pot measures six inches.

You may notice that plants from the nursery often come in plastic pots with almost a dozen holes at the bottom. These pots provide excellent drainage and make it easy for the nursery workers to water hundreds of plants at once without worrying about whether any one plant gets too much water. If you purchase a plant that comes in this type of pot, I recommend that you keep it in that pot for at least a few weeks before repotting.

Whatever pot you purchase should have at least one drainage hole at the bottom. The larger the pot, the larger the drainage hole should be or it should have more drainage holes. Imagine a big pot with a tiny drain hole. It would take forever for the water to drain, and the hole would likely become clogged with soil.

Next, we want to consider the material the pot is made of, and whether it will allow the soil to breathe. Ceramic is the least breathable pot material because the glaze covers all the pores of the clay used to make the pot. Terracotta is more breathable but can become fragile after years of watering since it is more porous. I've had terracotta pots that break when I try to move them after a few years of watering.

Now, if your heart is set on a pot because you think it is pretty, but it might not be the best material or has no drainage, there is another option: use it as a cache pot. A cache pot is a decorative pot that you put another pot inside of. It looks like your plant is growing in that pot, but actually, a second, smaller pot is holding the soil and the plant. Just make sure that the inner pot has good drainage and is made of a breathable material. I like to put my plants inside plastic pots, and then use a ceramic or terracotta pot as the cache pot. When it is time to water your plants, simply remove the inner pot from the cache pot, water the plant thoroughly, let it dry and place the inner pot back in the cache pot.

A bigger pot isn't always better

As plant parents, we can be eager for our plants to grow so we might buy a big pot thinking, 'If I give my plant more room to spread its roots, it will grow faster'. But a big pot will not help plants grow faster.

Think about it like this: you wouldn't buy a baby bigger clothes if you wanted them to grow faster. You might buy slightly larger clothes so they can grow into them, but if you put a baby in an adult suit, they will probably get lost in the fabric. The same concept applies to plants.

When you put a small plant in a pot that's too big, two things happen. First, you are likely to overwater it because there's so much soil. The roots will soak up a small portion of the water, and the rest will remain in the soil. When there's more water than the roots can soak up into the stem and leaves, the soil will remain soggy, which will attract mould and potentially lead to root rot.

The second thing that can happen is that the roots will keep expanding, but there will be no new growth above the soil. If your plant has an easy time growing new roots beneath the soil, it won't spend as much energy growing its leaves and stems above the soil.

The key for growth is finding a pot that is only slightly bigger than the previous pot. We want there to be a little bit of room for the roots to expand, but not so much extra space that there will be excess water that the roots cannot soak up within a day.

The benefits of terracotta and grow bags

Whenever people ask me what my favourite pots are, I usually say terracotta pots or grow bags. Because terracotta pots and fabric grow bags are slightly porous, they allow air to move into the pot and around the outer edges of the soil. Roots naturally stop growing when they come into contact with open air, which is known as 'air pruning'. When the edges of the roots are air pruned, the plant is encouraged to grow new branching roots, leading to a healthier root structure.

Preparing to repot

Before we repot our plant, we want to prepare our space and prepare the new pot. The first thing that you need, of course, is a new pot to move the plant into. Most of the time, we are 'up-potting' our plants, which is when we move our plant into a larger pot to make room for more root growth.

But sometimes, you may find yourself needing to move your plant to the same-sized pot or even a smaller pot. For example, if your old pot breaks, but you see that the roots still have room to grow, you may want to find a similar-sized pot. Sometimes you may even find that your plant has a difficult time absorbing all the water in the soil, in which case you may want to move your plant into a smaller pot.

Repotting plants involves working with loose soil, so it can be messy. Much like when I water my plants, I prefer to repot my plants out on my balcony where it is easy to clean up any stray soil. Whether you repot your plants inside or outside, you can use a gardening mat to catch any dirt.

Once I lay down my mat, I also gather all the supplies I need so that they are within reach:

- The plant (already in original pot or grow bag)
- Pot that the plant will be moved into (make sure the new pot has a hole, or a few holes, at the bottom)

- Soil
- Fertilizer, nutrient sticks or other nutrient mix
- Khurpi or other flat tool for tilling and loosening soil
- Gravel or other loose material to create a drainage layer
- Gloves, especially when working with spiny plants like cacti

When I have all these items within reach, I put on a pair of gloves and prepare the new pot with a layer of gravel. It's best to put a one-inch layer of gravel at the bottom of the pot so that the holes don't become clogged with soil over time. Once we have everything ready, it is time to get our hands dirty! (Unless, of course, you are wearing gloves.)

How to repot your plant

If you're planning to repot your plant, do not water it. Let the soil and the roots dry out over a couple of weeks. It is easier to work with dry soil than it is to work with wet soil.

When we repot plants, we have to be careful not to disturb the roots. If your plant is root-bound, then it has probably become quite snug in the pot, but we want to make it easy to slide out with very little effort.

The first thing I do is separate the soil from the pot by taking my khurpi or any other flat tilling tool and sliding the tool between the outer edge of the soil and the inner edge of the pot. Then I move it around the outer edge of the pot until the soil feels loose.

Once the soil has been loosened, I put one hand on top of the pot, above the soil, and use my other hand to slowly turn the pot upside down. I'm careful, treating my plant much like we would a baby. They are, after all, our plant babies!

If the soil is loose enough, your plant should just slide out of the pot and into the palm of your hand. If you are repotting a plant that came from the nursery in a plastic bag, simply make a slit in the plastic and carefully remove the plastic layer.

Do not **pull the plant out of the pot. If you pull and tug on your plant, you could damage the roots and stem, and may even separate the roots from the plant, which will be difficult to fix.**

Once you have removed the plant from its original pot, you will find that there is a ball of soil surrounding the roots. As we water the soil and let it dry over and over, the soil becomes compressed, and the roots begin to grow secondary and tertiary hairs that cling to the soil, so it all comes out in a ball of soil and roots.

Do we break off some of this old soil or keep it intact?

Breaking the soil could damage the roots, especially the finer hairs. When I have a large root ball, I carefully try to break off some of the soil around the edges. Sometimes you can gently knead your fingers along the outside of the soil ball and excess soil will fall off. Be careful not to apply too much pressure or tear the soil away. I might also use my khurpi, gently inserting it into the soil around the root ball so that the outer layers of soil can crumble off on to my gardening mat. I keep working around the soil ball until I see roots, and then I stop. Even if there is soil clinging to the primary roots, I leave it. Although the roots may still be covered in old soil, I know that they will grow and extend in the new pot.

After you have prepared the new pot with a layer of gravel, you are ready to put in the plant. Carefully flip the plant over, placing one hand on the bottom and another hand on top to keep the plant stable. Gently slide the plant into its new pot, on top of the gravel.

You will notice that you have not yet put new soil into the pot. Right now, you are checking to see where the plant sits in the new pot. You want to leave about an inch of space from the top edge of the pot to the top layer of soil. If you do not leave some space at the top part of the pot, the soil will not retain water because it will flow out of the top of the pot rather than sinking and soaking through the soil. A small gap also gives you room to till the soil for aeration.

When you put the plant in the new pot on top of the layer of gravel, you will notice that the base of the stem sits a few inches below the top edge of the pot. You want to put enough soil in the pot to raise the plant so that the base of the stem sits only an inch or so below the top edge. So take the plant out of the pot and add a few inches of fresh soil. I like to keep the old pot nearby so that I have a place to keep the plant while I put soil into the new pot.

After adding a bottom layer of soil, you can put the plant back into the new pot and see where it sits. If it looks like the base of the stem is still a little lower than you want it, you can break some soil off the root ball or add a little more soil. If the soil is too high, you can take some out or dig a little hole to give the plant more room. Now that you have adjusted the soil, the plant sits right where you want it to. Right now, the plant is sitting on top of the soil, but it cannot hold itself up until you cover the roots by adding more soil.

With one hand, hold the plant straight, and with the other hand, begin to add soil. If the plant is tilting a little to one side, add soil to fill that gap and help the plant stand up straight again. You can use a small gardening shovel to add soil, but I like to use my hands. Keep adding soil evenly around the plant until the pot is filled up about halfway. At this point, stop and gently press down to compact the soil around the plant, but be careful not to press down too hard. A light touch is all you need.

By pressing the soil down, you compact it and build a solid foundation for your plant. Then keep adding soil until the pot is filled up to about one or two inches from the top. Leave more space for bigger pots and less space for smaller pots. The bigger the pot, the more water you will use to water it thoroughly, so you will need more room for the water to sit while it drains into the soil. Gently press the soil down again and make sure that your plant is stable and standing up straight.

Once you are happy with how your plant looks in the new pot, give it a thorough watering to help the roots expand into the new soil. It's important to keep the soil moist for the first two weeks to encourage the roots to grow in all directions.

Six steps for potting a plant

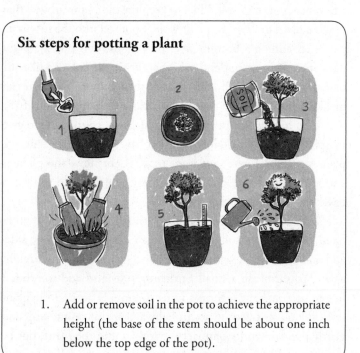

1. Add or remove soil in the pot to achieve the appropriate height (the base of the stem should be about one inch below the top edge of the pot).

2.   Balance the plant in the centre of the pot.
3.   Evenly fill the pot with soil until the pot is about halfway full. Make sure to cover the roots.
4.   Press the soil down.
5.   Add more soil until it fills up to an inch or two below the top of the pot.
6.   Water thoroughly.

After repotting your plant

After repotting and watering your plant, you might notice that the soil sinks down. This is normal because there are air pockets that the soil sinks into when it is saturated with water.

Do not try to adjust the wet soil. If you try to adjust the soil while it is wet, it will create a slippery, clay-like surface, which is not good for your plant. Let the soil dry over the next couple of weeks and till it. If you feel that the soil is still too low in the pot, it is okay to add a fresh layer of soil on top as long as you leave some space so the water doesn't flow over the top of the pot.

Now that your plant is happy and watered in its new pot, move it to an area where it will get a good amount of light. Continue to give it love and attention.

Recap: Repotting your plant

Reasons to repot:

- Your plant has outgrown its pot
- Pests have infested the soil

- Your plant is in a pot that is too big
- The roots are infected

Signs that your plant has outgrown its pot:

- Roots coming out of the top of the soil
- Roots growing out of the drainage holes
- You hit roots at the surface when you till the soil
- Your plant has brown, crispy leaves despite regular watering

Pots serve three purposes:

- Pots are decorative
- Pots provide a drainage system for our plants
- Pots hold the soil and the plant, allowing the plant to stay contained while also allowing it to get fresh air

Bigger pots aren't always better.

Be careful to get the right-sized pot for your plant. If the pot is too big for the plant, you could overwater it because there is too much soil. If the pot is too big, you may also not see the top of the plant grow as much.

Six steps for potting a plant:

1. Add or remove soil in the pot to achieve the appropriate height (the base of the stem should be about one inch below the top edge of the pot).

2.   Balance the plant in the centre of the pot.
3.   Evenly fill the pot with soil until the pot is about halfway full. Make sure to cover the roots.
4.   Press the soil down.
5.   Add more soil until it fills up to an inch or two below the top of the pot.
6.   Water thoroughly.

After you repot your plant, let the soil dry. After a few weeks, till the soil. If the soil has sunk down, it is okay to add a fresh layer of soil on top.

5

Spreading the Plant Love: Plant Propagation

I love propagating plants because it makes it easy to share the joys of plants with others. Propagation essentially means growing an entirely new plant from part of another plant. When you think about it, it's neat that many plants have the ability to grow a new plant from just a leaf, a stem or a part of the root.

Sometimes my friends and family are interested in plants, but they might be hesitant to go to the nursery and pick out a plant of their own. Maybe they don't have a lot of time to go to the nursery, or they feel too intimidated to shop for plants. If you are buying your very first plant, going to the nursery can be overwhelming.

Giving your loved one a plant baby that came from one of your own plants saves them a trip to the nursery and is a great way to encourage them to learn about gardening and get started on their own plant journey. It's also fun and makes me feel like a plant grandfather.

Another reason you may want to propagate plants is to experiment. Say you have a plant that's become big and happy in its pot, but you want to see how it looks in another pot, or want to have the same type of plant in another room. But your plant already looks so big and happy in its old pot! You don't want to move it.

No problem. We can take a little piece of that plant and try making a new one to put in the other room or try something new with it.

How to propagate plants

Different families of plants are propagated in different ways. Wanderers, for instance, can be propagated with any part of the vine that contains a node for aerial roots. Storage houses with fleshy leaves, such as snake plants and succulents, can be propagated using only part of the leaf. And some plants can only be propagated with part of the root system intact, or need a bulb from underneath the soil.

There are three steps to propagating plants: **cut**, **root** and **transfer**.

With all propagation, the idea is to **cut** off part of the plant; provide a growing medium such as soil, coco peat or water to **develop roots**; and once the roots are long enough to anchor the plant, **transfer** it into a new pot. Depending on the plant, these steps can happen in a different order. For example, we can air layer the plant, which is when we encourage the roots to grow at a node *before* we cut and transfer that part of the plant.

Plant propagation checklist: Tools and other useful items

- Bypass pruners (or sharp scissors)
- A sharp knife or razor
- Khurpi (or another flat tool for tilling soil)
- Small shovel
- Bottles or other containers for rooting plants in water
- Spray bottle
- Soil
- Shallow pots for rooting
- Bigger pots for propagating many plants at once
- Table
- Gardening mat (propagating plants can be messy!)

General guidelines for propagation

No matter what kind of plant you are propagating, there are some universal truths to keep in mind.

First, when we propagate a piece of a plant, we want to make sure that the end placed in our growing medium was the end that was closer to the root on the original plant. If we flip the exact same piece upside down and plant it, the piece will be much less likely to propagate. We want to orient the piece in the soil the same way that it was oriented before.

Second, for storage houses, we should always make sure the plant forms a callus before trying to root it. Callus refers to hardening of soft tissue at the end where a cut has been made. If the plant is holding moisture and is not yet callused, it can become infected and won't propagate.

Additionally, propagation takes time. Some plants may take six months to propagate, so this is a long process.

Finally, there is no guarantee that a plant will always propagate new plants. Even if you follow all the rules exactly, you are still going to have some plants that just don't grow new roots. The best way to increase your chances of successfully propagating your plants is to try to propagate many plants at once. For some plants, this means taking multiple cuttings. For others, it means trying to get several different nodes to develop roots at the same time.

The etiquette of asking for plant cuttings

If you are feeling adventurous and don't mind starting with a baby plant, you may want to start with a cutting. Let's talk about proper etiquette when it comes to asking for cuttings.

Always ask for permission before taking a cutting. People spend a lot of time caring for their plants. It's not polite to start hacking away at someone's plant without permission. If you are passing a garden and see a beautiful plant and would like to get a cutting, just ask if it would be all right to take one. Most gardeners are generous and want to see others grow their own plants, so they will more than likely be happy to share one with you.

If it is a plant in a park or other public space, make sure that you are not damaging the plant or other plants to get the cutting.

Sometimes you can ask a nursery for cuttings, and they will be happy to help. Most nurseries sell plants that are more mature and are happy to provide cuttings because it gives them a chance to connect with someone who gardens and will come back later for pots, soil and more plants.

Make sure that you cut at the right spot. You need to make sure that the cutting includes the nodes from which new roots can develop while propagating. We will talk about how to make a clean cut and propagate plants later in this chapter.

While starting from a cutting does require more time and work, it is a great way to begin gardening if you're on a budget.

Self-propagating plants

The easiest plants to propagate are those that do most of the work themselves by growing new root systems underneath the soil. Since the rooting is already taken care of, all we need to do is take the plant out of the pot, make a cut to separate the root systems and transfer the root systems into separate pots.

Self-propagating plants include:

- Snake plant
- Spider plant
- Pilea
- Aloe vera
- Dracaena
- ZZ plant
- Rain lily
- Caladium

Let us take a look at how some of these plants self-propagate and the best way to cut and transfer them when they are ready.

Snake plant

The snake plant is a good example of self-propagation. The larger snake plant leaves are from the original plant. Next to these large leaves are smaller snake plant leaves poking out of the soil. The snake plant made an entirely new root system to sprout a second plant! What's even more amazing is that the original snake plant wasn't happy a few months ago. Her leaves were drooping, so I moved her into a pot with new soil and fertilizer and nursed her back to health. Now, she is so happy that she made a little baby plant, too!

My snake plant made new roots first. Now we need to separate these two plants at the root level. First, I take my khurpi (or any other thin, flat tool) and loosen the soil around the edge

Root systems of mother snake plant and baby snake plant

of the pot like we would if we were going to repot the entire plant.

Once the soil is loosened from the pot, I flip it and use my hand to catch the plant. No pulling! If we rip the roots, we will hurt the plants.

I can now see how these plants are joined near the roots. Using my fingers, I gently massage the edges of the soil ball to break away some of the extra soil until I can see more clearly how the roots are entangled.

There is one horizontal root going from the original snake plant to the new one. We need to carefully cut this root with a sharp bypass shear and transfer the cutting to a new pot. It's very simple! Once the two plants are separated, I can plant the original snake plant in the same pot and move the new snake plant pups into a new pot to give to a friend.

Spider plant

The spider plant is another plant that does most of the work for us. If you take good care of your spider plant, you will notice that it throws out little 'spider babies' (they are smaller spider plants, but I like to call them spider babies). At first, they look like flowers, then they grow into little plants that look like the main plant.

To propagate spider plants, we can simply use our bypass pruners to cut the baby spider plant from the long stem that connects it to the mother plant.

You will notice that there are nodes where the baby plant connects to the stem.

There are two ways that we can encourage these nodes to develop roots. The first is to simply place the cutting in water

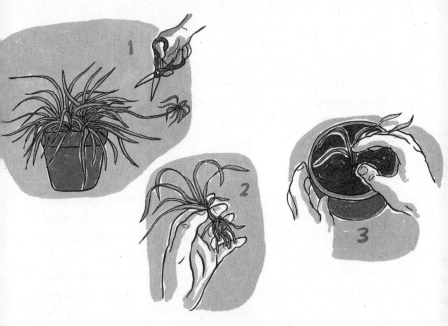

Steps to propagate spider plants

for a week or two. We don't want to submerge the entire cutting in water, only the bottom part where the nodes are. You may need to find a container with the right-sized opening where the plant can sit on top with only the nodes underneath the water. After a couple of weeks, you will notice roots forming, and then you can transfer this baby spider into a pot of fresh soil.

The second way to encourage roots to grow from the nodes of our baby spider plant is to place it directly in the soil after cutting. For this method to work, we need to keep the soil damp. It's best to use a smaller pot because we are only trying to encourage roots to grow, so we do not need to water the soil as thoroughly as we normally would. Instead, we want to keep the surface layer of soil wet.

What I do is take my spray bottle and spray the top layer of soil until the area around the spider babies is moist. We want to keep this pot in a shaded area so that it stays moist, and I might spray it every day so that the soil doesn't dry out. Like the spider plant that we put in water, we can move it after a few weeks once there are a few long, healthy roots coming out of the plant.

Dracaena

Dracaena is another popular species of plant that self-propagates. If you're not sure what kind of plants fall under dracaena, think of the Song of India. Similar to snake plants, healthy dracaena plants will often create a new root system underneath the soil, and we will see a new stem coming out above the soil. If there's a gap between the mother plant and the new stems, it is simple to take the plants out of the pot, cut the horizontal root connecting the two plants and repot the pups in a new pot. If the baby stem grows out close to the mother stem, the process can be trickier. Just be careful not to damage the root system and look carefully for the one root that connects the two plants before cutting.

ZZ plants and other rhizome plants

Most plants with rhizomes, or bulbs beneath the soil, can self-propagate. The biggest difference between self-propagating rhizome plants and self-propagating plants like snake plants is that we divide the roots differently. The rhizomes underneath the soil are essentially where these types of plants store water, which is why plants like ZZ plants and bamboo can go a long time without being watered. With rhizome plants, we need to make the cut between each bulb. Consider each bulb to be a separate plant and cut the horizontal roots connecting the bulbs.

ZZ plant bulbs/rhizomes

Once you have each bulb separated, you can plant them in their own pots.

If you are new to propagating plants, I recommend starting with self-propagating plants such as the snake plant, spider plant and dracaena. All these plants have a high success rate, so they are a great way for beginner gardeners to learn how to propagate.

Plants that propagate from the stem

With some plants, it's possible to grow an entirely new plant from only a part of the stem. It's quite amazing when you think about it. Imagine being able to grow an entire body from just your arm or your leg! I find that plants that can be propagated with just the stem are fairly easy to work with, but they do require some patience and have a lower success rate than self-propagating plants. Typically, plants that can be propagated with just the stem have a higher success rate right after their blooming season.

Plants that can be propagated from a stem cutting include:

- Dumb cane
- Song of India
- Dracaena
- Syngonium
- Money plant
- Wandering Jew
- ZZ plant
- Jade

Dumb cane

Dumb canes are among my favourite plants to propagate. I have found that you can take a hopeless-looking dumb cane stem and turn it into a happy, thriving plant. You may be wondering why they call these plants dumb cane. It is because if you chew on the plant, you can temporarily lose the ability to speak due to the juices in the plant that can irritate your mouth and throat and cause swelling. Please do not chew on your dumb cane plant!

During the first few months of the COVID-19 lockdown in India, I was searching through old pots and found a dumb cane stem that looked dead. What's amazing about some plants is that they can appear dead, but with enough care and patience, you can save them, bring them back to life and maybe even encourage them to grow new plants! In the case of the dead-looking dumb cane that I found, I cut the stem into three pieces. Two out of the three pieces grew roots and leaves. So how did I do this?

I did the same thing with all three dumb cane stems, but one of the stems did not grow roots or leaves. This is an important lesson: sometimes you can do all the right things, but the plant might not propagate. Every plant has what I've been calling a 'success rate', which is the probability that a cutting will successfully grow into a new plant. Because no plant has a 100 per cent success rate, it is always a good idea to try propagating a few cuttings at once to increase your chances that at least one cutting will become a new plant.

You will observe brown rings around your dumb cane stems. Each ring is a node, and therefore a potential new dumb cane plant waiting to be grown.

Stem propagation step 1: Make a clean cut, leave out to dry and form callus

The first thing I did with my hopeless dumb cane stem was that I made a clean cut using a sharp knife. I made sure to cut pieces that had at least one or two rings around them.

Unless you have a long stem that you wish to cut into several pieces, you only have to slice a small piece, about three to five centimetres, off the end. After you make the cut, you will notice that the cut end of the stem feels wet. Most plants that can be propagated from their stems store water in their stems, which is why the stem of the dumb cane is thick and tough, almost like bamboo.

After making the cut, it's important to let your dumb cane stem sit out in the open air for at least a day. After a day or so, you will find that the end of the stem has dried and hardened, forming a callus or barrier. It is important to wait for a callus like this to form before propagating any plant with a fleshy stem that holds water because it prevents the stem from developing rot when you attempt to propagate it.

Stem propagation step 2: Let the cutting sit in water or soil

Once the stem has formed a callus, it is time to try to make it grow roots. You can either plant the stem in soil or let it sit in water. I find that putting the stem in water works better because the roots grow faster, and you can see the root growth. If you are a beginner, I recommend starting with water. Not only will you have a greater chance of success, but you can also see if it is working with your own eyes.

In either water or soil, you only need to cover a few centimetres of the stem, including the callus. In water, I may place a few dumb cane stems standing up with the callus side down in a container and fill it with three or four centimetres of water. In soil, I would only bury the callus and stem about three centimetres deep. If you are rooting your stems in soil, make sure to keep the top layer of soil moist for the first couple of months. I like to spray the top layer of soil every day when I'm rooting stems in soil.

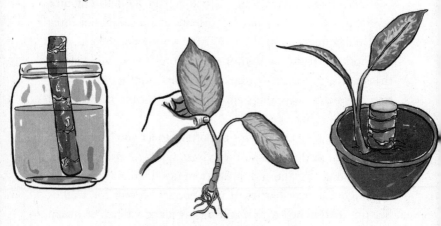

(Left) Dumb cane stem left in water for four weeks
(Right) Dumb cane stem left in soil for four weeks

The rule of nodes: Any stem with nodes can be rooted in water

If you're wondering which stems and plants can form roots in water, the answer is very simple: anywhere you see a node is an area where roots can form if they have moisture. Nodes are any bumps or segments that join two parts of the stem together. On dumb canes, you will notice rings around the stem. These are the nodes. On a money plant, you will notice bumps on the stem, which are also nodes. Any stem with nodes can be placed in water, and there is a chance that it will develop roots.

Stem propagation step 3: Move to soil

If you're rooting your stems in water, you should move the stems to soil when you notice about two centimetres of root growth. It is important to move your stem to soil before the roots get too long because the root structure that forms in soil is different from the root structure that forms in only water. If you moved your stem to soil in step two, you can skip this step and simply wait until you notice growth. Once your cutting is in soil, give it a thorough watering. Remember, our goal is to get the stem to keep growing long, healthy, happy roots, which means we need to give it plenty of water for the roots to search for.

How do we know when our stems have long roots? When we see new growth on top. The more growth we see on the top of the plant, the longer the roots have grown into the soil.

When you move your stem into soil, it is okay if it only has a little bit of space. Our goal is to see new growth, not to grow a big plant. In fact, I like to propagate many stems in one pot at the same time so that I can increase my chances of successfully propagating a few plants.

Other plants that can be propagated with a stem cutting

When propagating wandering plants from the stem, the same rules apply:

1. Cut off a small section from the bottom of the stem and let it develop a callus.
2. Develop roots in water or soil.
3. Move to soil and keep soil wet until you see new growth.

These steps work for any plants that store water in their stems, including the Song of India, dracaena and syngonium. **But make sure that you are using the stem!** Sometimes it is easy to confuse the stem with the stalk, especially for plants like syngonium. The stalk is the part of the plant that connects the leaf to the stem. *Stalks cannot be propagated* because roots do not form out of the stalk of most plants. Stems, on the other hand, have nodes. So if you see a node on a part of a plant, then you know it is the stem, which we can potentially propagate.

How often should we change the water when rooting stems for propagation?

When we are rooting stems in water, one question a lot of gardeners have is, 'How often should I change the water?' I recommend changing out the old water for fresh water every ten days to replenish some of the dissolved oxygen and to ensure that the plants do not rot.

When you replace the water, it is important to not just dump the water out. Just as when we are repotting our plants, we want to be careful not to disturb the roots. Remember, these are new, baby roots. They are soft and delicate like a baby.

The trick to changing the water is to use one hand to hold the stems and carefully tilt the container so that the water flows out slowly. Take your time. You don't even have to empty out all the water, only about half, and then slowly pour in new water. Try not to use a high-pressure faucet. Just fill a bottle or watering can with fresh water, and slowly pour in enough water to cover the base of the stem where the roots are forming.

Air layering: Rooting before we cut

Now we know how to propagate a plant by first taking a cutting, helping it develop roots and then placing this new plant in soil. But what if we want to make a plant develop roots before we take a cutting?

You may be thinking, 'Is this the same as self-propagation?' It is a good comparison because we have to wait for these self-propagating plants to develop new root structures and bud off into new plants before we cut them.

But what about wanderers and stiff and sterns that don't bud off into new plants below the soil? Is there a way to get these plants to develop root structures for new plants while they are still connected to the mother plant?

There is a way, and it is known as air layering.

Air layering might sound a little confusing at first, but we have already learnt some of the main ideas. Think back to the 'Types of Plants We Grow at Home' section of this book. We learnt that we can use wet paper towels or a moss stick to encourage aerial roots to grow on wanderers such as money plants and Wandering Jews. With air layering, we are using the same idea: make the roots grow out of a node or branch, and then cut off that part of the plant and make a new plant.

There are a few different methods to air layer plants, so let's look at how each one works.

Air layering method #1: Pin the stem to the soil

One way to air layer plants for propagation is to simply use the soil already in the pot to encourage the nodes to grow roots, which is also known as 'soil layering'. This method works only for wanderers with flexible, non-woody stems.

It is a good idea to use a wide pot so that you have plenty of soil on the surface to keep pinning the stem down as it grows. What we do is take the stem of a plant and lay it over the soil. Then we take two pins (I like to use bobby pins) and place a pin on each side of the node. What we are doing is securing the node of the plant to the soil so that the plant thinks, 'This is a good place for me to start growing roots.' Be careful not to push the stem down too hard or use pins that squeeze the stem. We still want the stem to be able to carry water from the roots to the leaves, so we need to make sure that we are not cutting off its circulation.

Continue to pin down as many stems as you like. Remember, to increase your chances of success, you should pin down many nodes.

Once the stems are pinned down and the nodes are touching the soil, we need to keep the soil moist. Grab your spray bottle

Money plant stems pinned to soil for air layering

and spray the top layer of soil. You may want to spray the soil twice every day to keep it moist. After a few weeks, you will notice that some of the nodes are now rooted to the soil. Once the nodes are growing roots, remove the bobby pins. I usually take the bobby pins out of the soil after a week or two.

Give these roots a month or two to grow. Once the roots are long and healthy, you can cut the stems before each node, carefully dig up the new root structure, and have new money plants to share with your friends and family! Of course, if you just want a bushy money plant, feel free to leave these new roots in the soil, and you will notice that your plant will keep growing longer stems, which you can continue rooting back into the soil.

Plants that can be air layered in potted soil include:

- Money plant
- Wandering Jew
- Jade

Air layering method #2: Rooting on branches with pouches of soil

Air layering in the soil is easy for wanderers. But what if we are trying to propagate stiff and sterns with rigid branches that are far away from the soil? We cannot simply bend the branch down to the soil, as the branch would break. Instead, we need to bring the soil up to the branch.

Stiff and sterns typically have a layer of bark around the branch. If we look at a curry leaf plant, we can see small bumps along the branch. These are the nodes where roots can grow. But since there is an outer layer of bark, the first thing we need to do is scrape away some of that rough outer shell. Take a knife and gently scrape away the bark around the nodes. You don't need to scrape hard. Just a very light rub of a sharp knife should peel away the outer layer of the branch.

Using a blade to scrape away bark around curry leaf nodes

Plastic bag of potting soil tied around a branch for propagation

Underneath the bark, you will see that the branch is green and fleshy, similar to the inside of a dumb cane stem. The next step is to cover this part of the branch with soil. What I like to do is take some coco peat or potting mix and place a handful on a piece of plastic wrap. I then spray the soil with water until it has a dough-like consistency—moist, mouldable and sticky. I then roll the soil into a ball, mould it around the branch that I just peeled and use the plastic wrap to secure the soil around the branch. The plastic wrap also helps keep the soil moist. If you find the soil is drying out that may mean the wrapping was not secure enough or had holes. You may need to open the plastic wrap and make sure to fill it with moist soil, and tie it better this time. You can use twisty-ties or rubber bands to secure the plastic wrap and soil around the branch.

After about three weeks to a month, roots will start to form inside the soil pouch. Once the roots begin to grow from the branch, you can cut it off the stiff and stern and place it in a pot with soil where it will grow into a new plant. This method of air layering is popular in nurseries for growing new stiff and sterns and even some blooming wonders like hibiscus. In nurseries, you might even notice stiff and sterns with bags of soil secured to every branch so that they can potentially turn one plant into a few dozen!

Common plants that can be air layered from the branch with soil include:

- Curry leaf
- Hibiscus
- Lemon tree
- Bougainvillea
- Fiddle leaf fig

Both methods of air layering have a high success rate because of the simple fact that the new plant you are trying to form is still connected to the main plant. It is still getting all the water and nutrition it needs to develop its own roots, so it doesn't have to work as hard to become a new plant.

Propagating from a leaf cutting

Did you know that some plants can be propagated from just a leaf? When I first learnt this, I was amazed. But it makes sense if you think about it; if leaves can store water and contain chlorophyll to gather sunlight, then they should be able to grow into an entirely new plant. The biggest difference between propagating from a leaf as opposed to the other types of propagation is that it takes a lot of time. If you are making an entirely new plant from the leaf, the biggest keys to success are patience and propagating many leaves at once.

Plants that can be propagated from a leaf cutting:

- Snake plant
- Aloe vera
- ZZ plant

The rules for propagating a plant from a leaf are the same for most of the plants listed above. First we cut the leaf, place the leaf in soil or water with the bottom side facing down and wait for roots to form. I'll explain how it works using a leaf from a snake plant.

The first step to propagating a plant from a leaf cutting is to cut off part of the leaf. For snake plants, I use a sharp knife to cut a leaf off close to the base of the plant.

Steps for snake plant
leaf propagation

Cutting out snake plant leaf for
propagation

Once we have the leaf, we can cut it into smaller pieces. I find that it is best to make a cut every three or four centimetres. **Remember which edge of the cutting is the bottom edge.** The bottom side of each cutting has the highest success rate of growing roots. Some of the middle segments might confuse you since they look the same on the top edge and the bottom edge, so when you make each cutting, make a mental note of which side is facing down.

You can also cut the bottom edge of each leaf segment into an upside-down 'v' shape to increase the surface area. Sometimes this helps increase the chances of the leaf developing roots.

After you cut the leaf into several pieces, take a pot of soil or a jar of water and place each leaf segment in it with the bottom edge facing down. It is a good idea to wait for a day after cutting for callus to form, before inserting the cut leaves in water or soil. Even though you can propagate leaves in both water and soil, I find that I have a higher success rate using soil for leaf cuttings.

If you do start to propagate the leaves in water and notice that no roots are forming, you can try moving them to soil.

When you place the leaves in the soil, firmly press the soil around the leaf so that it has support and can stand upright. I also like to propagate around a dozen or two dozen leaves at the same time so that I have a higher chance of successfully propagating multiple plants. If you have a big pot and a few different types of leaves you want to propagate, it is fine to use the same pot, just make sure that it is big enough to hold all the leaves you are trying to root.

After you place the leaves in the soil, spray the top layer of the soil with water. Like all rooting that we do in soil, it is important to keep the soil moist to encourage roots to grow.

Remember, propagating plants from leaf cuttings takes a lot of time. I have had some leaves grow roots within three months, and in some cases, it has taken eight months for roots to develop. Continue to spray the soil with water every week, and be patient. Eventually, you will see new pups appear from the soil, which you can move to separate pots and share with your loved ones.

Recap: Spreading the plant love: Plant propagation

Propagating plants is when you take a part of a plant and make an entirely new plant. Plant propagation is a great way to learn more about your plants, make more plant babies for free, and share the joys of plants with your friends and family!

The two key things to remember about propagation are:

- Be patient
- Start with a lot of cuttings

No plant has a 100 per cent success rate for propagation, so you're going to fail sometimes. By starting with many cuttings, you increase your chances of successfully growing new plants.

There are three basic steps of plant propagation:

- Cut
- Root
- Transfer

Not all methods of propagation go in this order, though.

Self-propagation

Self-propagating plants are the easiest to multiply. Simply wait until you see enough new growth above the soil, carefully remove your plant from the pot and separate the main root structures. Self-propagating plants include snake plant, pilea and dracaena. Rhizomal plants like ZZ plants also self-propagate.

Propagating from stems

Some plants only need the stem to be propagated. These plants include all wanderers, and dumb cane. First get a stem, slice off the end, let it form a callus, then encourage the stem to grow roots in water or soil. Once the roots have developed, transfer the plant to a pot.

Air layering

Air layering is when we encourage the roots to grow before cutting the plant. Air layering works on wanderers like money plants as well as stiff and sterns like curry leaf and hibiscus. We can air layer directly into the soil, or attach bags of soil to the branches of plants after we remove the bark around the nodes. Once the roots develop on the plant, you can cut off the branch or stem segment and move it into a new pot.

Propagating from a leaf cutting

Some plants, like the snake plant and aloe vera, can grow new roots from a leaf cutting. Simply cut the leaf into segments and place the leaf segments *bottom side down* into soil or water. If you are using soil, keep the soil wet. Propagating a leaf takes a lot of time, so be very patient. Once the leaf develops roots, you can move it into its own pot.

Propagating is a game of patience! But the rewards are high: free plants for you and your friends!

6

Ideas for Plants Inside

Why do people take care of plants in their homes? Many gardeners have houseplants because they love the way plants look and enjoy the companionship that plants provide. Plants come in so many lovely shapes, colours and textures that people often use them to liven up their homes. Indoor plant arrangement has become a central part of interior design, and many from the younger generations have been drawn to plants because they see amazing pictures on social media of homes decorated with elaborate figs and monsteras.

More practically, we bring plants inside because we have more control over our indoor spaces. Most of us can control the temperature with the AC and adjust the airflow by opening a window or closing a door; we can also set up lights or use blinds to adjust lighting. Outdoors, we don't have as much control, so our plants are often at the mercy of weather conditions. For instance, heat waves, cold winds, floods or droughts can easily kill plants in an outdoor garden, but if they're inside, we can keep them warm and give them water no matter what the weather decides.

Some casual gardeners, like my mother, enjoy having plants inside because it gives them something to focus on and tend to while they go about their day. My mother enjoys watering her plants while catching up with friends on the phone. So, in a way, houseplants are great for people who enjoy multitasking or want something to do inside their homes.

I personally enjoy plants because they are my thoughtful companions. By taking care of them every day, I have grown attached to my plant babies, and in turn, they have taught me many lessons about patience, perseverance and growth.

Because urban areas are becoming more densely populated, having a yard or an outdoor garden has become somewhat of a luxury. But if there's no space outside your home to grow plants, no problem. We can easily grow plants indoors with a pot, water and some soil.

Whenever I bring a new plant into my home, I think about where I will keep it. I consider what would make it happy. It is like the beginning of our friendship. When you actually look around your home, you'll be surprised by all the nooks, crannies, ceilings and surface space you have that plants can enjoy. In nature, a plant stays in one part of the ground. Inside, plants live in a pot and can be exposed to different levels of light. You set up a space just for them. With enough ingenuity and imagination, even people living in tiny apartments can find room to grow a miniature forest.

Deciding which rooms are best for different plants

Earlier, in Part I of this book, I explained why there is no such thing as an 'indoor plant'. There are just plants that can survive and thrive in low levels of light.

Our homes vary in size, arrangement, furniture, humidity and lighting. What works in one home may not work in another. What works in one room may need adjusting in the room next door. Different plants will want different things, and different rooms will offer those plants different opportunities to grow, so you may have to move your plant babies around to find what is right for them.

I have rearranged my plants and my rooms more times than I can remember. I find decorating and moving plants throughout my home to be meditative and comforting. Bringing nature inside connects me to my childhood and my home, yet reminds me to stay in the present as I take care of my plants.

Moving plants around can also be good for them. In nature, a plant might have to fight to get light or risk dying in the shade of another plant. Inside, we have more control. We can help the little guy. By giving plants even just a few extra hours in a brighter area, I can make sure they are getting all the light, water and attention they need to be as happy as possible.

I find that grouping plants by how much light they need is an easy way to keep track of when to water and aerate specific groups of plants. For example, keeping all my bright shade plants on the patio helps me remember that they need to be watered more often. The low-light plants I keep in my bedroom don't need as much water. Grouping my plants also makes it easier for someone else to care for my plants when I need to travel. I can just tell them, 'Keep an eye on the plants outside. They might need watering while I'm gone. But the plants in the bedroom should be fine without much attention.'

Almost any plant can be grown in almost any home, as long as it is able to get the light it needs to be happy. Here is how I like to think about my space, figure out which rooms are best suited for my plant babies, and how I arrange my plants so they can feel more at home.

Plants that spice up the kitchen

I love to keep plants in my kitchen. Cooking, much like gardening, is a peaceful practice. Both are productive activities that can calm us down. And plants are a big part of our diet. A lot of what we eat comes from plants! Not every home has enough space to grow an entire garden full of fresh food, but we can all grow something that can spice up our cooking.

Herbs such as basil, rosemary, coriander and mint are great for beginner gardeners. Microgreens of mustard, methi, broccoli and radish are also easy to grow, and if you use them in your cooking, you will naturally pay more attention to them.

Some of the world's best chefs agree. Celebrity chef and Master Chef India judge Ranveer Brar and I spent some time discussing how the plants in our pots are related to the food on our plates.

'Cooking and gardening are so interconnected. The meaning of cooking changes once you know where your ingredients come from,' Brar said. 'Herbs and leafy vegetables are the easiest to grow, maintain and use in meals, and growing them fresh can have a big impact. The quality of ingredients affects the flavour of a dish.'

There are often lots of good little spaces to grow plants in our kitchen. If you have a window with bright light in the kitchen, it might also be a good place for aloe vera and other plants that can help sanitize or heal small cuts or burns. Even the most graceful cook can sometimes nick themselves or touch something hot while preparing a meal, so having an aloe plant handy can be nice.

If your kitchen space is limited and you are worried that a plant might get in the way, but still want a plant in your kitchen, you can hang it from the ceiling. Also pay attention to any unused corners or shelf space. A corner, shelf or even the top of the fridge can be an ideal place to keep plants like a spider plant that doesn't need a lot of attention. I don't recommend tucking your first plant into a corner, though; you want to keep your first plant in a place where you can see and remember it so you can create a habit of gardening. So if you are arranging mainly for decor, make sure you have some practice and are already an adept plant parent.

Bathrooms, kitchens and other little rainforests

Money plants are good to keep on top of the fridge. They love light! Kitchens have more light than you think, and we tend to keep our kitchen lights on more than the lights in other rooms of our homes. Kitchens generally have an overhead light, and light that may come in through a window or from an adjoining room.

Plant cuttings in planters to add greens inside homes

Kitchens and bathrooms have another thing plants love: humidity. I like to put a shelf above the sink where my wanderers can hang and enjoy the humid environment. If you have space by the sink or build a shelf, you can keep any plants with nodes nearby, and the water in the air will encourage the aerial roots to grow. And because these rooms have sinks, it is easier to clean up any mess.

You may be thinking, 'Okay, so I should keep plants that like water in these rooms,' and that is one way of looking at it. But remember, you are more likely to overwater your plant than underwater it. So if you keep your plants near a water source, don't let that be an excuse or an urge to water them more often than they need. Just test the soil and water them normally or maybe even a little less frequently and let them enjoy the humidity.

Because kitchens and bathrooms are extra humid, they are not a great place for storage houses such as snake plants, succulents and cacti. Keep storage houses in other rooms.

Plants that help us relax in bedrooms and bathrooms

Bedrooms and bathrooms are supposed to be calming spaces, and plants can help make these spaces feel peaceful. One reason I like to keep plants in my bedroom is that I love it when plants are the last thing I see before I go to bed and the first thing I see when I wake up. Being surrounded by plants makes me feel closer to nature and reminds me of how beautiful our natural world is.

Lavender plants open up our nasal passages, helping us take deeper, calming breaths, which can help us get a good night's sleep. Lavender plants grow well in bedroom windowsills that receive direct light.

I have found that people like to hang a sprig of eucalyptus from their showerhead when they take a hot shower. The steam releases essential oils in the eucalyptus that both invigorate our nervous system and relieve stress, so hanging eucalyptus in your shower is great whether you prefer morning showers to wake up or nightly showers to wind down! A eucalyptus sprig or lavender plant can also make the bathroom smell better.

It is important to note that *lavender and eucalyptus are both toxic to cats and dogs*. So if you have pets at home, you may not want to keep these plants or be very careful to keep them away from your animals.

Another plant that does well in bedrooms is the money plant. Some people use money plants to create a natural curtain on their windows. The plant gets plenty of good light while also providing some shade for the person who takes care of it.

Making memories with our living-room plants

Living rooms are both comforting and lively. On one hand, they are where we relax after a long day. On the other hand,

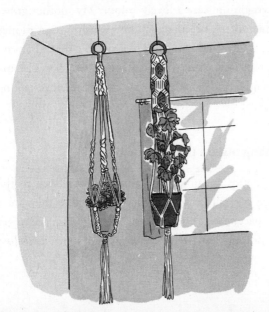

Plants hanging on macrame hangers inside homes

the living room is where we come together to talk, play games and spend time with our family and friends. Plants naturally fit right in. They comfort us by reminding us to be patient and move slowly, but at the same time, they are alive and are always growing . . . as long as we take care of them.

Because living rooms tend to be spacious and often receive the best natural light in our homes, they are an ideal place to grow larger plants such as monstera, fiddle leaf figs and large snake plants. I like to arrange a few together, careful to make sure each one gets enough light. They need plenty of space to stretch their limbs. Large plants in a living room feel like a backdrop to family life. They always remind me of when my mother would have Keerti and I pose for pictures in front of money plants, syngoniums and areca palms in our living room. I can already hear her saying, 'Get closer to your sister, Vinayak! The palm is blocking your face!'

Plants in a living room also spark some of my favourite conversations. When I have guests over, they will say something like, 'Those syngoniums are a lovely colour. My mother grows syngoniums like that!' or 'Look at how bushy your money plant has gotten! How did you get it to grow like that?' I always appreciate a plant that offers a good story or two between my family and friends. And what plant parent doesn't love talking about their plants?

Plants that hang out on the balcony or patio

Balconies and patios are unique because they are open to the outside but are typically well shaded. And because they are a semi outdoor space, patios and balconies are a good place to get messy with repotting and watering. Dropped some dirt? Just sweep it off. Spilt some water? Wipe it once with a towel or just let the sun evaporate it.

Plants love the bright shade of a balcony. It's like going to the beach; they get an opportunity to soak up the sun, which encourages them to drink up their water, photosynthesize and grow. I like to water them and leave them, then rotate them out when they have had their fill of water and light to let a different group of plants enjoy the same treatment.

My balcony is also separated from my indoor space, so it is an ideal place to keep plants when they are fresh from the nursery. When they are out on the balcony, I can check on them to make sure they are not carrying diseases or pests that could spread to my other plants. I also keep my compost bins out there so my house doesn't smell like banana peels.

I like to keep fruit trees such as lemon, papaya and fig on my balcony (though remember that it can be a challenge to lug big pots upstairs). You can guide wanderers up towards a tree, too. I do that on my balcony so my money plant feels it is climbing to the canopy of a rainforest. Mehndi and coriander also enjoy indirect sun on the balcony as they germinate. I also grow holy basil and lemongrass on my balcony because I like both lemongrass and basil in my tea, and the lemongrass helps keep away the mosquitoes. On the weekend, my balcony gets extra crowded as I bring some plant babies out to visit for a few hours and enjoy the view and some extra light. It's like a plant party.

Keep in mind how shaded your balcony or patio is and which direction it faces. If your patio faces south and there is nothing around to block the sun, it might be a little too toasty for some of your plants, especially in the afternoon heat. If you think your patio is too bright, consider using an umbrella or patio furniture to add some shade in which you can keep your plants. Try things out. Even if something doesn't work, that is okay. You will learn, and this is your space to make your own. Experiment.

Of course, be mindful of the weather, too. If it is too hot or too cold for the plant, it will not enjoy its balcony experience. No plant likes to be in weather that is too hot or too cold for it, or outside during a natural disaster. Bring your babies indoors.

Co-working with plants

Have you ever gotten into a good work groove? When you have a home office, it is important to limit distractions to be productive. At the same time, it is important to take breaks. I typically work for fifty minutes and then take a ten-minute

Plants around work desks

break to clear my mind before getting back to work. I find that when I take a break to watch a video or have a conversation, it is more difficult to get back into my workflow because then I am thinking about what I just watched or talked about when I should be focusing on work. But when I shift my focus to a plant, it is easy to shift my attention back to my work tasks, helping me establish a nice, productive workflow.

Plants also offer our eyes a nice, calming break from our screens. Looking at a screen for hours on end takes a toll on our eyes. We feel teary-eyed, sore and in severe cases, can have a pounding headache from staring at a bright screen. Of course, you should make sure to turn down the brightness of your screen and install a filter to make your screen less harsh to look at. But I also find that giving my eyes a break from my screen to stare at my plants makes me feel a lot better.

To be honest, all plants make pretty good work buddies. I keep quite a few plants in my office, but then again, I work with plants. Before I became the 'Lazy Gardener', I liked to keep a few plants on my desk that I could admire throughout the workday, and maybe even rotate or prune whenever I took a break. You may enjoy blooming wonders that give your workspace a nice aroma and are pleasant to look at. Or you might prefer storage houses, which are low maintenance and minimize distractions.

Think about what you like to be surrounded by and play around! It's okay to change up the plants in your office, and it may even be a nice way to find new sources of creativity.

Organizing your tools and supplies

As you get into gardening and start to care for more and more plants, you will find that you have quite a lot of gardening

Essential gardening tools

supplies, such as pots, watering cans, misting bottles, aprons, bags of soil, loose cuttings, khurpis and gloves. You may start to wonder, 'Where am I going to keep all this stuff?!'

Worry not. You have several options. Many gardeners like to keep a box or build a shelf where they can keep their gardening supplies. I personally like to keep a lot of my gardening supplies near my plants so that they are accessible, and I don't have to search for a tool when I need it. I also find that when I keep my tools and supplies near my plants, it reminds me to use them. When my tools are hidden away in a toolbox, I may notice that one of my plants needs pruning, but will think, 'I don't have time to find my pruners. I will do it later.' And then I might forget. But if my pruners are close by, I will trim my plant then and there.

Of course, you may not want to have all your gardening supplies scattered around your home either. Eventually, you will find that there is an area of your home where you tend to take care of your gardening tasks. For me, my balcony is where I water most of my plants and change out the soil, so I like to keep my pots, watering cans, gloves and bags of soil out there. If you don't want to leave your gloves and tools scattered on a table, you can hammer a few nails into the wall to hang them from. You can also install nicer hooks or a peg board, but I find that a nail or some thumbtacks work just fine.

If your plants are scattered throughout your home, it may be a bit trickier to organize. But generally, you can think about which tools, bottles and soils you use on each plant and try to keep the necessities near the plants that need them. So if you keep wanderers such as money plants or monsteras inside your living room, you may want to keep your misting bottle on a nearby shelf so you can easily reach for it and mist those aerial nodes throughout the day.

Every gardener develops their own system over time. You will eventually discover what works best for you.

Plot how you pot: Using pots to streamline your practice

As I mentioned in the 'Finding the Right Pot for Your Plant' section of this book, pots serve as decor and provide some control in terms of how much or how little water and air our plants' roots receive. But as you begin to have multiple plants, you can get creative with how you use pots to take care of them.

For example, you may want to colour-code your pots so you know which plants need more water and which ones need less. Another thing you can do is keep your plants in a pot with a good drainage system and put that pot inside another pot without a drainage system—a cache pot. When it is time to water your plants, you can carry the cache pot outside, remove the inner pot, water it, let the water drain and place it back in the cache pot to be carried back inside. I like this method because it keeps my plants' drainage system intact and prevents water from spilling on to the floor of my home.

As your plant babies grow into plant teenagers and plant adults, you may want to begin taking cuttings for propagation. I like to keep a few different sized pots around my home to propagate plants in. If you are propagating plants in water, then you may want to keep a few clear bottles in which to root plant cuttings. With clear bottles, you can observe the root growth and know exactly when they are long enough to transfer the cutting into a pot of soil. I even propagate plants on the door of my fridge using magnetic planters!

Smaller pots are, of course, easier to move than larger pots. Keeping plants in smaller pots is nice because I can take them outside to get a little sunlight. My biggest struggle as a gardener has been large, heavy pots. I love my large plants, and I want to keep some inside. But I used to dread having to water my large indoor plants. I would either have to put a towel underneath or strain my back trying to move the pot outside (always lift with your legs). The worst situation would be if my large plant died. How would I move it out?

Recently, I've discovered 'planter caddies', which are round discs on wheels that make it easier to move a giant pot around your home. So before you go potting a stiff and stern like a fiddle leaf fig or rubber plant in a huge, heavy pot, you may want to invest in a planter caddy so that you can move your large plant around as needed.

As you up-pot your plants, you will likely have some leftover pots. These old pots make great hand-me-down pots for new, smaller plants to move into! Reusing pots or making pots out of household items is good for the environment and saves you money.

Make the most of your light

Common knowledge tells us that we should place our plants near a window or outside because they need sunlight. But that's a bit of an oversimplification. Any light source, including light bulbs, table lamps and light reflected off a wall or a mirror can be used by plants for photosynthesis. All light helps! There is no need to depend on the window alone.

Many of us have large tube lights in the kitchen, which are great because they send diffused light throughout that room. On top of a shelf or a fridge is a good place to keep low-light plants so they can enjoy the diffused light and use it to make food while you're raiding the fridge. And when it's a partly cloudy day, you can always take your low-light plants from the kitchen out onto your balcony so they can enjoy some natural light.

Table lamps and reading lights are also useful. If you add a small bulb to a dark corner, you can make the room much more comfortable for your plant babies.

We also need to remember that light reflects and bounces off the walls, furniture and mirrors in our homes. Dark colours absorb light, which means there will be less light for your plants in a dark room surrounded by dark furniture. A white room will reflect the most amount of light, so there is more for your plant in a room with white walls. You can also use mirrors to redirect light.

Because the sun moves through the sky, you may not be able to set your mirror up in one position and reflect direct sunlight all day long, but it can still add extra light to a room or rooms by reflecting ambient light.

Some factors that will affect how much light mirrors add to an area include:

- The size of the mirror(s)
- The number of mirrors
- The size of your window(s)
- The direction your windows are facing
- The size of your room

Generally speaking, more mirrors and larger mirrors will add more light, and south-facing windows will receive the brightest light. So if you have a north-facing room with a few mirrors, it could be a good set-up for low-light plants. And if you have a room with a south-facing window and a large mirror, only place plants that need bright light in that room.

So how do you make the most of the light in your home? Think like a plant! Do the pen test from the 'Light' section of this book, and make sure your plants have access to a good amount of light throughout the day, but aren't in direct, hot sunlight for extended periods of time.

Make the most of your plants

What plants you decide to keep inside will depend on your personal preferences and how you organize your space. I keep many different plants inside and see lots of ways to use them in different spaces. Wanderers are so versatile, especially syngonium. My syngoniums are happy inside or outside, in water or soil, and can be grown to be green or pink. I love them no matter where they are grown, how they are grown or what colour they are.

How we set up our home is part of what makes us who we are. How you decide to arrange plants in your home will be unique to *you*. Maybe you like to keep your plants near water because it is easier for you to take care of them that way. Maybe you would prefer to arrange creepers crawling up an outside wall and set up hanging plants that can zigzag across the house.

My only rule for myself is to keep my plants in spots where I can easily check on them. If I keep a plant on a shelf, I make sure that it's not too high up, and that I can easily take it down to water it, prune it, aerate the soil and take care of it.

It is your choice, as long as you—and your plants—are happy.

Recap: Ideas for plants inside

Different rooms and spaces in your home can be ideal for different plants.

The kitchen is good for plants that can be used in your cooking and plants that like moisture, especially if you have a bright light. It's a good place to keep aloe vera for cuts and burns.

Bathrooms are great for plants that like moisture, including all wanderers.

Bedrooms are good for calming plants that you like to have around when you're trying to relax.

Common areas are good for plants that inspire conversation and for bigger plants (depending on light).

Balconies are a great place to keep plants because it is easier to clean them. You can keep a wide assortment of plants on balconies, especially plants that like bright light. If you keep your plants on the balcony, be careful that they don't get too toasty in direct light and bring them inside if you're in for bad weather.

The office is good for plants that are calming so you can shift your focus to them for a mental break during the workday.

List of common gardening tools and supplies:

- Pots
- Watering cans
- Misting bottles
- Aprons
- Bags of soil
- Loose cuttings
- Khurpi
- Gloves
- Bypass pruners
- Anvil pruners
- Garden mat
- Fertilizer and fertilizer sticks

Keep your supplies accessible.

You may want to hang some of your tools and supplies on the wall to remind you to garden.

Plot how you pot.

You can use different types of pots to organize your plants. You may want to colour-code your pots or keep similar pots together. It's also helpful to keep plants you are propagating together so you can check on their progress.

You may want to keep heavier plants on a planter caddie so you can move them around.

All light helps!

Any light source, including light bulbs, table lamps and light reflected off a wall or a mirror can be used by plants for photosynthesis. Just make sure the plant is getting the light it likes.

Remember your babies!

Keep your plants in spots where it is easy to check on them.

7

Building a Community: Propagating the Joy of Plants

'The best time to plant a tree was twenty years ago. The second best time is now.'

—*Chinese proverb*

We all have our own individual journeys as gardeners. We learn the joys of gardening, what our plants need and how to care for them. Gardening can be a mindful, solitary activity where we can find a sense of peace, as it is for me when I am pruning, repotting or generally tending to my plants. But gardening is also a wonderful group practice. When we care for our plant babies with other people, it helps us bond and shows us how to take care of our world and one another.

Do we grow plants or do plants grow us?

Gardening makes us wise. It teaches us the importance of being patient and nurturing the world around us. These are lessons that I want to share with other people because I believe that everyone can gain some wisdom from the practice of gardening. It is a timeless, borderless practice.

Any time in history, anywhere in the world, you can find people taking care of nature. I do find that more and more people are disconnected from the practice of gardening; we feel, 'There's a grocery store down the street. Why garden?'

But there's nothing that beats the feeling of getting your hands dirty and knowing exactly where your food came from because you watched it grow out of the earth. Even if we're growing plants to appreciate their beauty instead of growing herbs, fruit and vegetables, we're still learning about how our actions either help or hurt the natural world around us, making us more mindful of our choices.

I believe that the lessons that plants teach us must be shared. It is our duty to teach the next generation how to care for plants if we want to keep Mother Earth happy and green for generations to come.

Along my personal journey, I have met hundreds of gardeners who all find tremendous joy from plants. I have seen parents and children grow closer, neighbours rally to save parks and people form lifelong friendships due to their common interest in gardening. Seeing how much joy can be spread when gardeners of all ages and levels of expertise come together is what inspired me to start my own community, Lazy Gardener.

Building a community doesn't have to be a big, lifelong journey. Just like some gardeners may only have one plant while others have more than a dozen, I believe that sharing the joy of gardening with even one other person can make an impact.

As taught in the ancient art of bonsai, it is okay to start small, and it is okay to stay small. You might already have someone in mind whom you want to inspire to garden—a friend, family member, neighbour or maybe your children, and that's great! I want to encourage you and show you how to share the wonders of plants with the people in your life. And who knows? You might meet someone new.

Sharing plants with family and loved ones

Plants make excellent gifts. Even if your friends or family do not consider themselves gardeners, anyone can care for a plant and will enjoy having them around. I feel there is a plant for almost every personality and home. If you know someone who likes to have a natural remedy for everything, get them an aloe vera that they can use to treat scrapes and sunburns. Or maybe you have a friend who travels a lot. No problem! Get them a snake plant, which can go a long time without water. You now know enough about plants to choose the right plant for at least a few people in your life.

Gifting plants is special because they continue to grow, just like our relationships. Yes, you are giving somebody something that they need to care for, but I like to remind my friends, 'Hey, enjoy this plant and look after it. If it dies, that's okay. But I believe you can keep it alive.' I find that just that little encouragement helps people form a lasting bond with their new plant baby.

Everyone can benefit from having a plant in their life. Giving someone a plant as a gift is heart-warming for both you and the person you are gifting it too. It's a win-win: you have encouraged someone to garden, and they have received both a plant and a whole new world to be a part of. And it gives you an excuse to go to the nursery to pick out a plant (and maybe do a little shopping for yourself). Remember, your local nursery is part of your plant community, too!

Gifting and swapping plant cuttings

If you want to give your friends or family a more casual gift that doesn't cost a lot of money, give them a cutting of one of your plants! Sharing cuttings teaches both you and the person you are giving the cutting to about propagation, one of the most fascinating aspects of plants.

Swapping cuttings is a fun and resourceful way to collect more plants. Especially if your friends or family already grow plants, you might think, 'Oh, I wish I could grow that plant, too!' after seeing one of their babies. If it is a plant that can be easily propagated from a cutting, you can offer to trade for a cutting of one of your own.

I have even participated in swap events where a group of gardeners come together to trade a variety of their cuttings. Community cutting swaps are a great way to discover new plants and meet new gardeners.

Growing plants as a community

From farms and markets to parks and gardens, plants have always brought people together, and I believe that they will continue to bring people together as long as we take care of Mother Nature.

Plants were in many ways the glue that kept my family together. Yes, communication and sharing responsibility played a big role in my upbringing, but most of our chores revolved around plants, and after a long day, we would always find ourselves lounging beside our plant babies.

During my time at the monastery of His Holiness the Dalai Lama, I found that plants played a big role in cultivating mindfulness and tranquillity within the community of monks and fellows. And now, wherever I go, I find myself naturally gravitating towards other gardeners, or introducing people to the world of plants.

Chances are there is already a plant community near you, such as a community garden or other people who grow plants in their homes. As you advance along your journey as a plant parent, you will start to notice plants in people's houses, or plants in a park or a yard. As you notice people with plants, you can stop and ask them about what they're growing. I find that most people love to talk about their plants, and suddenly you've made a new plant pal!

Of course, the closest bond you can make with another plant person is growing a plant together. And one of the most rewarding ways to share responsibility for the caring of plants is with a community garden.

Setting up a community garden

Community gardens work well in neighbourhoods, apartment complexes or even on the rooftop of a condo. Sometimes you may need to ask for permission, but I think it is easy to persuade people to make space for a garden. Who doesn't enjoy fresh and delicious fruit and vegetables?

There are many means and methods of building a community garden. The first step is to plant the idea with your neighbours or family, saying, 'It would be amazing to grow some fruit and vegetables!' The biggest obstacle is typically space, but you can make a garden in just a few square feet if you plan it right. If you have only a small area, you can try vertical gardening or focus on growing microgreens and tomatoes, which require very little space.

Once you've gotten permission and have recruited some members of your community to help, it's gardening time! You may want to build planters, but you can also use an empty plot of land or repurpose some boxes, bins and old furniture into a garden. Just remember to make drainage holes if you're repurposing found objects.

From there, it is a matter of deciding what to grow, doing some research, planting the seeds and continuing to work together to care for your garden. Oh, and of course, enjoying the food you grow when it is ripe and ready to eat!

Easy plants to grow in a community garden:

- Tomatoes
- Cucumbers
- Squash
- Carrots
- Beets
- Spinach
- Eggplant
- Chillies
- Onions
- Bitter gourd
- Ladyfinger
- Lemons
- Oranges

Networking with gardeners online

The internet is another excellent place to meet new gardeners, exchange ideas and share advice. YouTube, Instagram and Facebook are all good places to meet a growing global community of gardeners. Remember that the gardeners you see online may live in different parts of the world and may have more or less experience than you, so what works for them may not always work for you.

In 2019, I started my own community for gardeners called Lazy Gardener. On YouTube and Instagram, I share plant tips and host live videos with guests, and I even share stories and answer questions from all kinds of gardeners. Search for Lazy Gardener, and feel free to tune in and ask me questions or share your journey with me. I always love to meet new gardeners!

The number-one rule for networking online is to be respectful. Gardening and working with plants should make us feel good, so it is always better to be gentle, kind and supportive with other gardeners online.

Social responsibility

The biggest thing that gardening has taught me is that we each have a responsibility to take care of our natural world. As you care for plants, you may become more aware of nature around you and more motivated to protect it. Actions both small and large can have a big impact on plants. I often find myself cleaning up trash and plastic bags from green spaces. I also pay attention when I see that a park is going to be converted into a parking garage, or when construction seems to intrude on a natural area that has plants that are older than you and I. And I feel the need to do something.

Working to save Shiva Vatika Park with fellow nature conservationists felt like the right thing to do, and I'm happy that we were able to preserve a natural area that would have been impossible to regain. I encourage you to be aware of when nature is endangered, and organize to challenge projects that go too far.

Simple, easy ways to be socially responsible:

- Start gardening!
- Start a community compost
- Organize a block walk to pick up trash
- Set up an appreciation walk through a park or along a trail
- Limit emissions by cycling, walking and carpooling
- Take care of the trees and plants in your neighbourhood
- Use canvas bags or reusable bags when shopping
- Reduce, reuse and recycle
- Purchase second-hand
- Advocate for the protection of natural parks and resources by writing letters to your municipality
- Research and advocate for green, sustainable energy practices

Activities for kids: How to teach your human babies about plant babies

Kids are naturally open and creative, and they will make up the next generation of adults that will take care of the earth (and hopefully us) when we grow old. One of the best things we can do for the environment is get kids excited about gardening.

Teaching kids about plants always takes me back to when my sister and I would explore our backyard, collecting creeper seeds and asking our neighbours for cuttings. Kids are naturally curious, so when we present something positive like gardening to them, it helps them grow and propagates something good for the world.

Plants teach kids profound lessons. We become a lot more grateful for the food on our plate when we learn just how long it takes to grow a plant. We learn to be patient and appreciate small changes by checking on our plant babies each day. We learn to be mindful and aware of our surroundings by focusing on the present. These are positive practices and shifts in perspective that we carry with us for life.

Working with plants is also very interactive. Most kids love getting their hands dirty, watching the water seep into the soil, and observing the slow but rewarding progress of their plants as they grow.

Actor Lakshmi Manchu once told me during a Lazy Gardener live session, 'I like to involve my daughter in hands-on activities that allow us to spend quality time together but also have fun. Gardening is one such activity. It's beautiful for your kid to witness the journey of the plant you planted that took on a life of its own.'

If you have kids at home, there are many gardening activities that you can do and some that you can start with just the food in your fridge!

Teaching children about vegetables with onions, carrot-top plants and celery

Growing vegetables inspires curiosity in kids. Because we can easily root them in water, they give parents and children a peek at how roots grow. As the roots grow, you can teach your children about primary, secondary and tertiary roots. You can also explain why plants grow roots to begin with; that when a plant senses water, it will typically grow roots to absorb it.

Why do plants need water? For photosynthesis! So this is also a great lesson on photosynthesis, or how plants make their own food. Vegetables store water in the part that we eat, which is why celery, onions and carrots are often juicy.

Growing different vegetables is also a chance to show kids the difference between taproots and fibrous root systems. This new perspective opens up a whole new world for kids to be curious about. 'What kind of root structure do those plants have?' they might ask as they look at different plants you grow at home or walk past in your society. From there on out, they will be more conscious of the experience of the plant beneath the soil.

Root vegetables also tend to grow faster than many other plants. They typically grow beneath the ground, and their roots grow relatively fast. They still take some patience; nothing grows overnight. But we often get to see faster growth than we normally would, which is great fun.

Like all propagation, there is still a chance that these plants won't grow roots. If propagation fails the first time, you can teach your kid that growing plants takes patience, and sometimes you have to try it a few times before it works. Don't be discouraged! Try again. This is a perfect lesson in perseverance.

Let's start with one of my favourite activities: rooting an onion.

Rooting an onion and making it grow shoots

When I was around six or seven years old, I remember rooting an onion with my sister. It was the first time I saw roots grow out of a plant. Keerti and I would check on our onion each day, and we would be giddy to see the roots getting a little bit longer. The roots in the water fascinated me, like thin tentacles growing out of the plant. It's amazing to see how elaborate plants are beneath the soil. We always see the leaves and flowers on top of the plant, but when we see this large root system underneath, we get a clearer picture of just how complex and wonderful plants are.

Rooting an onion in water is simple, and you probably already have everything you need.

What you need:

- Water
- Clear bottle, glass or jar
- Whole, raw onion—any type will do
- Toothpicks, nails or screws (only required if the opening of your jar is too wide to support the onion)

How to root an onion and make it grow shoots

Step 1: Fill your container with water. The onion should sit on top of the container such that the bottom, flat part of the onion just touches the water. If the onion is wider than the opening of the container, it should sit on top of the container.

If the onion is *smaller* than the opening of your container, you may need to push toothpicks, nails or screws into three or four sides of the onion so that it can be balanced on the lip of the container and float just above the water. Since nails and toothpicks are sharp, be sure to supervise and help your kids.

Step 2: Once the bottom of the onion is sitting in the water, place it near a window so it can get some light. Wait a few days, and you should start seeing roots grow!

Step 3: When the onion's roots are about three to four centimetres long, you can move it to soil and watch shoots grow out of the onion. If you plant your onion in early spring, you may even be able to watch it flower!

Tips

If you have multiple children, you can label each glass or jar with their names so that each child can watch their own onion as it grows roots. Be sure to keep the jars in an area of your home where your kids can easily check on their onions!

Rooting and growing a carrot-top plant

When we think about the carrot, we might think of a vegetable to be eaten as opposed to a houseplant we can care for and look at. But carrot tops are not carrots; they are the top of the carrot that is usually removed before eating the vegetable, not the tasty body of the vegetable we eat in our halwa. Carrot tops can grow fibrous roots but cannot grow into carrots once they have been taken out of the ground.

Why do carrot tops not grow into carrots? Because carrots are taproots. They grow from a small sprout of roots into the long orange vegetable we think of when we think of a carrot.

The carrot itself is the dominant root that takes in nutrients, continues to grow and develops smaller offshoot roots. Sometimes when you buy a carrot from the store, you can see these small hairs sticking out from the side or bottom of the carrot.

Even though we tend not to eat them, carrot tops can still grow to be lovely plants! Carrot-top plants are rich in colour, easy to plant and care for, and can show growth only a few days after you plant them.

Growing a carrot-top plant shows kids how to be sustainable and use every part of the plant. Kids may wonder, 'What other vegetable scraps can I grow into plants? What else can I reuse instead of throwing away?'

How to plant and grow carrots

What you need

- Water
- Small tray
- Kitchen knife
- Carrot

How to root and grow a carrot-top plant

Step 1: Chop off the top, leaving only two to three centimetres of the orange part and the greenery at the top of the carrot. Don't worry if your carrot top is bald and doesn't have any leaves–you can still use it.

Step 2: Fill the tray with water. Put the carrot top in the tray so that the foliage (petiole) extends upward into the air, and the edge that you cut is in the water.

Step 3: Place it near a window so it can get some light. Change the water every day or two. In less than a week, you'll see roots coming out of the bottom of the carrot top, and a little foliage hairdo growing out of the top. It will start to look less like the end of an old carrot and more like a plant of its own!

Step 4: When the carrot top's roots are about three or four centimetres long, you can move it to soil and continue growing it. Carrot- top plants grow up to a foot tall, and sometimes bloom little ornate white flowers that can light up your windowsill.

Tips

The carrot-top water may stain your containers, so avoid using your favourite mug or fine China and stick to a tray, jar or another similarly shallow container.

If you do not have a tray, you can use the same method we used for the onion by resting it on top of the water in a bottle, glass or jar, using toothpicks, nails or screws (if needed).

Rooting celery stumps and growing celery

Celery's signature characteristic is it long, sturdy green stalk. But did you know that the stump we cut off at the bottom can be used to regrow more stalks of celery?

Rooting and growing a celery stump is easy. It's a great activity for kids because they can eat the new stalks of celery, or they can put it on the sill with their onion and carrot-top plant.

What you need:

- Water
- Small tray
- Kitchen knife
- Celery

How to root a celery stump and grow celery

Step 1: Chop off the bottom, leaving about five to six centimetres of green above the stump.

Step 2: Fill the tray with water. Place the celery stump in the water so that the stalk-side extends upward into the air, and the bottom of the stump is in the water.

Step 3: Place it near a window so it can get some light. Change the water every day or two. In a few days, the celery will sprout leaves from the centre of the top of the stump. A few days later, you'll see stems and more leaves, as well as roots growing out of the bottom of the stump. Then, out of the stump will emerge walls of veggie: the stalks!

Step 4: When the celery's new roots are about three or four centimetres long, you can move the stump to soil and continue growing it. Celery plants are like little green giants; they can grow well over a foot tall!

Tips

There is no need to throw away the stalks you initially cut off the stump. You can either eat them after cutting them or put the bottom ends in cups, jars or glasses of water to snack on later. They will keep for a week or two, and you might even notice them grow a few inches, too.

Celery can be harvested after a few months, when it grows a bit beyond six inches.

If you do not have a tray, you can rest the stump on top of a bottle, glass or jar using toothpicks, nails or screws (if needed), just like an onion or carrot top.

Teaching kids how to grow their own food with microgreens

Microgreens are edible seedlings. They are great for children and beginners to start growing because they don't require soil and make a tasty addition to almost any snack! Microgreens are popular toppings on many dishes, and they are very nutritious, so they are great to feed your kid, too. (Maybe by growing green vegetables, you can get your children more excited about eating them. Maybe).

Microgreens can be grown from broccoli, methi, sarson (mustard), cilantro, beets, basil, kale and many other vegetables. In fact, the idea of growing microgreens is relatively new, so people are still experimenting and finding new vegetables that grow nice, edible seedlings. So don't be afraid to experiment!

For this exercise, I will focus on growing methi and sarson microgreens.

What you need:

- Water
- Small tray or container (a disposable food container works perfectly)
- Methi seeds and/or sarson seeds (any microgreen seeds should work)
- Paper towel or napkin (you can also use coco peat or soil, but a napkin works just fine)

How to germinate and grow methi and sarson microgreens

Step 1: Lay the napkin in the tray so that it completely covers the bottom of the tray. I like to fold my napkin once or twice before laying it down so there are plenty of layers to absorb and hold moisture.

Step 2: Spray the napkin with water. Do not get the napkin soaking wet. We just want it to be slightly moist. A few sprays of a spray bottle should do the trick. You can also dip your fingers in water and flick the water onto the napkin.

Step 3: Spread the sarson or methi seeds on the damp napkin. It is better to use a lot of seeds because we are only growing these plants to be baby-sized, not a full-sized plant.

Step 4: Spray the napkin and seeds with more water.

Step 5: Move the tray and seeds to a dark room with no light. You can also put it in a cupboard or cabinet, or cover it with a box. We want the seeds to feel like they are in soil so they will begin to grow. Once they sprout, they will look for light. By leaving them in the dark, we encourage the sprouts to grow longer in search of light.

Step 6: Mist the seeds with water every day. Once in the morning and once at night works best. *The seeds should always be moist.*

Step 7: After a few days to a week, you will notice sprouts coming through the seeds. Once you notice leaves growing on the stems, move the tray into the light so that the seeds can begin to gather light for photosynthesis.

To harvest, you can snip them right near the seeds with a pair of scissors. You can eat microgreens fresh by themselves, on a salad, or as a garnish on almost any dish.

Wait about a month before harvesting.

Step 8: Eat the microgreens and enjoy!

Tips

Instead of a napkin, you can also use coco peat or soil. Coco peat works well because it absorbs moisture but is sterile, so it won't grow (bad) fungi or moulds. If you do use coco peat or soil, add a small layer of the coco peat or soil on top of the seeds after spreading them out. Pat down the seeds and level out the coco peat or soil so that the roots can grow deep into the soil and give the plant additional support while it grows. I usually use the back of a spoon to level the soil.

Growing microgreens is an easy way to show children how to grow their own food. What's great about microgreens is that they can be grown during any season, so this is an activity for any time of the year.

I also like this activity because for kids, seeds are an amazing mystery. How does a tiny speck produce a plant? It seems like magic when they see something beginning to grow out of the seeds. This is a great lesson about how seeds germinate, or start to grow after being dormant for a long period of time.

You can explain that the seed won't grow until it is tucked into a moist, dark environment. First it will feel wet and think, 'I should grow roots,' and then it will sense the darkness and think, 'I should sprout a stem and leaves and find some light.' The process shows how plants naturally seek out water and light so they can begin feeding themselves.

In nature, seeds are usually put into the earth or fertilizer thanks to animals. Animals in the wild eat plants or fruit, digest the nutritional part of the fruit and then plant the seeds in the soil when they poop. But seeds can also be planted by gardeners or carried by the wind and dropped into the soil. There is a lesson in how seeds naturally propagate in the wild. In nature the seed plantation time coincides with the time that the plant creates fruit and vegetables. For the same reason, when you have a fresh piece of fruit, that is the best time to plant its seeds. Hybrid seeds have been modified for agricultural needs, but if you take seeds from any fruit or vegetable you are consuming, you can plant them right away, in the same season.

When we grow microgreens, we are replicating the natural conditions of the seedlings with the wet napkin and dark space. The difference between microgreens and most other seeds, though, is that they do not need external nutrition to sprout, which is why we can use just a wet napkin or coco peat. What we are witnessing with microgreens is the seed unlocking itself.

Although microgreens may look similar to one another, they vary in taste, so you can try them in many different flavour combinations.

Bon appétit!

Teaching kids about germination with rajma

Here's another activity that you can do with a few basic items that you may already have in your kitchen. I have typically seen this activity done with rajma beans, but any kind of dry bean will work.

We are going to plant about a dozen rajma beans in soil and allow them to sprout. Over the course of a week, we can dig up one rajma sprout at a time and observe the different stages of growth. Kids relate to this activity because they are in the process of growing a little bit every day, too.

What you need:

- Water
- Small tray or container
- Rajma beans (chickpea seeds also work)
- Coco peat or soil
- Spoon or khurpi (optional)
- Pen (optional)

How to sprout rajma beans

Step 1: Poke drainage holes in the bottom of the tray. Space the holes two to four centimetres apart.

Step 2: Fill the container with coco peat or soil up to one centimetre from the top of the tray. Level the soil with the back of a spoon or khurpi. You can also use your fingers.

Step 3: Poke holes in the soil that are about a centimetre deep. Make the holes in a straight line using a pen or your finger, spacing each hole a few centimetres from the last. Drop one rajma bean in each hole and fill in the hole.

Step 4: Spray the soil with water until it is thoroughly moist. *Coco peat needs more water than soil.*

Step 5: Place in a dark area, like a kitchen cupboard. You can also cover the soil with a thin layer of coco peat so you don't have to keep the tray in the dark, and your children can observe the growth.

Step 6: Water every day.

Step 7: Wait until half of the rajma seeds have sprouted. Each day, dig up a sprout. As you dig them up at different stages of germination, you can line them up from left to right in a place where your kids can observe the changes. After about a week, you and your children will have created a line of rajma sprouts, each at a different stage of germination!

Tips

This also works with chickpea seeds.
WARNING: Do *not* eat raw rajma bean sprouts. They can make you sick.

This is a popular activity in children's science classes because it shows children most of the stages of germination. Seed germination can be explained as when a plant breaks through the shell of its seed and works its way up through the soil so that it can begin taking in light and water and grow into a full-sized plant.

If you are a gardener, you may be hesitant to dig up seeds while they are still growing. But I love this activity for children because they are in the process of growing, too. I think it is important for children to see the different stages of growth so they can see that every day, the plant progresses and grows a little bit. This lesson gives children some perspective on their own growth, and they can begin understanding that growing anything—whether it is yourself or a plant or an idea—takes time, patience and care.

Teaching kids patience and care by growing a citrus tree

Growing lemons takes more time and patience than growing microgreens or watching rajma sprout, but I find that kids love to have a tree that can continuously grow fruit—especially lemons. Expect this to be a project that will take a year or two to see actual lemons, but once the tree is growing, you can keep it for a lifetime.

Keerti has a lemon tree for Mili, and she loves to collect the lemons from the ground. I also find that kids enjoy how sour lemons are; they can play a game with their friends to see who can suck on the lemon juice without making a sour face. And what's great about growing lemon trees is that you don't even need to buy the seeds because you can get them straight out of a lemon you have at home!

What you need:

- Water
- A ripe, fully grown lemon
- Knife
- Paper cups, or a tray, egg carton or other container
- Soil
- Six-inch or twelve-inch pot

How to grow a lemon tree from a lemon at home

Step 1: Extract the seeds from the lemon. Normally, we are used to cutting through the middle of the lemon to get two even halves, but we *do not* want to cut through the middle of the lemon when extracting seeds.

Instead, cut the top quarter off the lemon, and then use the tip of the knife to make a slice through the peel on top of the lemon. Then, you can use your fingers to pull back the peel and dig through the lemon to pop out the seeds without damaging them. I find this is the best method for getting all the seeds you need out of only one or two lemons.

Step 2: Cut a few small holes in the bottom of the cup or container for drainage. *Only adults should handle sharp objects.* Fill each container with soil. If you are using paper cups, fill almost to the top of the cup, leaving about a centimetre of space for water overflow.

Step 3: Sow (plant) lemon seeds in paper cups, tray or another container. Using a pen, pencil or screwdriver, poke holes into the soil about three or four centimetres deep. If you are using small paper cups or an egg cart on, I like to put two seeds per cup or two seeds per compartment where each egg usually sits. If you are using another container, make sure the seeds are spaced a few centimetres from one another.

Step 3: Place the cup near a window and keep the soil moist. You do not need to fully water the soil; simply spray it with water about twice a day.

Step 4: Wait for the seed to sprout. Once you see a stem growing through the soil, the seed has germinated.

Step 5: Once the stem is a few centimetres long and you begin to see leaves growing, you can transfer the baby lemon tree to a larger pot. Start with a pot that is about six inches in diameter. We want to keep our baby tree in a pot that fits its current size to avoid overwatering. As it grows, you can move it into a larger pot.

Step 6: Care for the lemon tree as a family. Once your lemon tree is growing, apply the concepts you have learnt so far in this book: water it thoroughly when the soil is dry, keep it in bright light, and prune when necessary. After a year or two, your lemon tree will begin to grow lemons, and you and your children can proudly say, 'We grew this from a seed!'

Tips

- Most citrus plants are easy to grow. You can also do this activity with oranges or limes.

- Lemon trees like their roots to be slightly cold, so avoid black pots if possible.
- Start with a dozen or two dozen lemon seeds to increase your likelihood of success.
- Lemon trees enjoy plenty of light, so a south-facing window is perfect.
- During the summer, you can move your lemon tree outside. Be careful to give it a gradual change, though. Lemon trees enjoy about eight hours of sunlight during the day, and to be cool at night. About eighteen degrees Celsius is a perfect night-time temperature for most citrus plants.

Growing a lemon tree can be a lot of fun and highly rewarding. I find longer activities like this that take years to see results are even more satisfying because of the time and patience they require—an important aspect of any serious gardening practice. There are quite a few lessons that you can teach your children along the way, such as the role of light and water, and how to water plants correctly. Remember how important drainage is and be sure to teach your children; no gardener is too young to learn about the dangers of overwatering plants!

You will also notice that lemon seeds vary in size. The larger the seed, the deeper it should go into the soil. This is true for almost all plants: big seeds live deep in the soil because they will grow into big plants. Small seeds should be closer to the surface because they will be small, and they need to be able to reach sunlight fast as they sprout through the soil.

Growing a fruit-bearing tree with your children is a special activity that they will likely remember for the rest of their lives.

The tree grows with them, and they can watch it mature over a couple of years. And once they have lemons, they can share them with their friends and encourage them to grow lemon trees of their own.

Turn anything into a pot

For a final activity, I want to encourage you to experiment with potting plants in all kinds of objects. Anything can be a pot! All it has to do is hold soil and a plant and be able to drain water. I've seen plants grown in broken clocks, bottles, desk drawers— you name it, and someone has probably tried to grow a plant inside it!

You may have to assist your child in drilling holes in the bottom of whatever they decide to grow a plant in. Once you have a good drainage system (several decently-sized holes in the bottom of your makeshift pot), simply pot your plant and take care of it.

Ideas for objects that can be turned into pots:

- Birdcage
- Broken guitar or sitar
- Tin can
- Old appliance
- Broken clock
- Desk drawer
- Teapot
- Bottle
- Suitcase
- Hollowed-out television or stereo

- Fish tank
- Toaster
- Toy truck
- Sideways bookcase
- Old tub or sink
- Cooler

Reduce, reuse, recycle: Making a water bottle vertical garden

Water bottles make great pots. They are easy to find, easy to make holes in, and with a little creativity, you can make them look really interesting! You can hang them to create a vertical garden, which saves space while allowing us to grow more plants. I love these vertical water bottle gardens because they allow us to water multiple plants without wasting any water.

Innovative ways to recycle things at home to grow plants

What you need:

- Plants with shallow roots, such as money plant, jade, portulaca
- Plastic water bottles
- Long hanging rod
- Rope or string
- Knife or scissors
- Paint or other supplies to decorate the bottles

How to make a water bottle vertical garden

Step 1: Find a place where there is already a sturdy, horizontal rod, like a pipe or rail. You can install a rod, or you may know a spot that is just right and is already set up. It is not difficult to find a bar that will work. For example, you could use the rail on your balcony fence.

Step 2: Cut off the bottom portion of all the water bottles so that only the top half of the bottle remains. We can turn the remaining half upside down and use the mouth of the bottle as a drainage hole.

You can also turn the bottle on its side and cut it horizontally to make it look like a boat, which will create a wider opening for plants. If you use this approach, you will have to poke holes in the bottle on the 'bottom of the boat' so that water will drain.

Step 3: Pot your plant babies in the bottles.

Step 4: Tie strings or rope around the bottle so it can be suspended and the plant stays upright. If you use a long rope, you can hang the bottles one on top of the other so that when you water the one on top, it drains down into the bottles below. The water runs through multiple plants, and the set-up saves you time, too!

Tips

Remember to pot your plants carefully so the roots are kept intact, just as you would with any other pot. Take a bit of time to hang the bottles carefully. You don't want the bottle to tip and your babies to take a tumble, especially off your balcony! Keep the garden somewhere where water can drain out underneath, and conform it to your space as needed.

There are numerous ways to create vertical water bottle gardens. Feel free to experiment! You can use larger bottles for larger plants or make different cuts to see how they turn out. Look online to see how others have done it, and enjoy the challenge of making your vertical garden unique.

Recap: Building a community: Propagating the joy of plants

Gardening is a great practice to share with others: friends, family and loved ones.

It's also a great way to meet new people.

Ways to bond over gardening:

- Gift and swap plant cuttings
- Garden as a community
- Network with other gardeners
- Advocate to protect nature
- Introduce the next generation of children to gardening

Ways to preserve and protect nature in your community:

- Start a community compost
- Organize a block walk to pick up trash
- Set up an appreciation walk through a park or along a trail
- Limit emissions by cycling, walking or carpooling
- Take care of the trees and plants in your neighbourhood
- Use canvas bags or reusable bags when shopping
- Reduce, reuse and recycle
- Purchase second-hand
- Advocate for the protection of natural parks and resources by writing letters to your municipality
- Research and advocate for green, sustainable energy practices

Good gardening activities for kids:

- Regrow root vegetables such as onions, carrot-top plants and celery
- Grow microgreens
- Germinate rajma
- Grow a citrus tree
- Create a vertical garden
- Turn almost anything into a pot

8

The Gifts of Gardening: Stories from Plant Parents

How plants helped me honour the lives of my parents

By Diti

My mother died a few winters ago. She had been paralysed for twelve years, and my husband and I had taken care of her throughout. Every year around her birthday, I still feel an emptiness that I never felt when she was with us.

When she passed away, I decided to keep her *asthi* with me. I already had my father's asthi from when he passed away eight years earlier. My husband and I bought a BIG pot in which we could put their asthi together. We bought two plants, a balsam and a celosia, and named them after my parents. They were my first plants.

In Bengali, we call plants *gaach* (গাছ), and we named them Maa Gaach and Baba Gaach. It was as though after all those years, they were together again. We were very emotional and happy.

Unfortunately, our happiness didn't last long. To prevent our twenty-seven rescue animals at home from damaging our plants, we kept these plants tucked away under a staircase where they received no light. We watered them like the person at the nursery told us to, but that turned out to be too much water. The pots were also too big. Maa Gaach and Baba Gaach started to look sick.

We were shattered. All the grief I felt when my mother and father passed away came back to me. But I didn't give up on the plants. I became determined to save Maa Gaach and Baba Gaach.

I started reading and watching videos about gardening. Slowly I started learning things. I shamelessly bothered a lot of people (including Vinayak!) for advice about how to be a better plant parent.

We cleaned and created a place on our small balcony and moved the plants there. To our despair, our senior dog started eating them. It felt like someone was biting my own flesh. I was shattered again.

Then, I watched a video about how to revive dead plants. I followed the instructions and ordered fertilizer sticks, which became a lifesaver for me and my plants. They slowly started coming back to life and are still happy today.

I hope that one day I'll have a balcony full of happy and healthy plants in honour of my parents.

How plants supported me during motherhood

By Keerti (Instagram: @indianfitmom)

Towards the end of 2016, I became pregnant with Mili. That Christmas, my work team received a poinsettia as a gift from one of our clients. Over the next few months, nobody took care of it. By March it was dying and slated to be thrown out, so I asked if I could take it home instead.

I planted it in our garden. I didn't take care of a lot of plants, but I grew up with them; my mother and brother both loved to garden. I wasn't sure if the plant would flourish, but I kept nurturing it.

At the time, I was six months pregnant and having complications. I had bleeding and severe cramps for thirty-six hours and was admitted to Stanford Children's Hospital where I was kept under observation for a day. Ultimately, the doctors said that they couldn't do anything; we would just have to wait and see. So they sent me home.

I couldn't sit for thirty-six hours. Standing was the only position that was comfortable for me. I kept looking at the poinsettia in my garden while pacing my living room.

The cramps stopped after a week, and I resumed work after my medical leave. On my return to the office, my co-workers behaved as if I had gone on a holiday. They were cold and distant. One of them asked me, 'How are you?' Usually I would remain formal and simply say, 'I'm doing great!' but that day, I was honest and said, 'I am not okay,' simply because I wasn't.

Later I overheard them gossiping about me. I spent the rest of my pregnancy in absolute silence—a silence that was broken by my daughter's cry when she was born in July.

From the time I returned to the office to the time Mili was born, I shared my deepest feelings with only my daughter and the poinsettia.

Now, my daughter Mili and I nurture plants together. I want her to have a connection with gardening because it is so much more than what it appears to be on the surface. Gardening is a life-changing endeavour that not only teaches you patience but also gives you a chance to see beyond daily frustrations. Plants teach me something every single time I interact with them. I want Mili to have this ability to connect with nature and learn from it.

If you want to teach your children about life, teach them how to garden. They will learn everything there is to learn in this world—faith, hope, courage, success, failure, resilience, persistence, humility and confidence.

Today the poinsettia is flourishing in my garden.

It taught me faith.

It listened to me when others wouldn't.

It gave me hope that everything would be all right.

It supported me when human beings didn't.

This plant saved my life.

Thank you, dear poinsettia.

Frequently Asked Questions

Frequently asked questions about adopting plants from a nursery

How long should I wait before repotting my plant from the nursery?

I usually wait about ten days before repotting new plants to ensure that they have acclimated. It may take more or less time for your plant to adjust, depending on the plant and how bright or dim the light is. Try to keep your plant in a similar type of light that it was in at the nursery. Plants that came from the shaded area need shade while plants that came from direct sunlight should be placed in direct sunlight. The best way to tell if your plant is happy and ready to be repotted is if you see new growth.

If my plant comes from the nursery in a plastic bag, should I repot it immediately?

While you can repot your plant right after bringing it home, I personally recommend that you wait a week or two, even if the soil and roots are in a plastic bag. If the plant could survive at the nursery in a plastic bag, then it can survive the same way in its new home. In fact, it might be easier for the plant to adjust if it stays in the plastic bag for another week or two.

Do not disturb the root ball when you tear away the plastic. If the roots get damaged, your plant will struggle.

The same advice applies to plants that come in polyethylene pots. You can leave your plant in the polyethylene for a week or two while it adjusts to your home. Be sure to continue watering your plant as needed.

While repotting, should I use the same soil that came with the plant? Or should I use new soil?

When your plant is ready to be repotted, it's best to change the soil, and choose a soil that is natural to that plant.

It's important to note that some nurseries use sticky soil or clay so that it's easier to lift the plants and move them around the nursery. If your plant came in sticky soil or clay, it's best to repot it with loamy soil, depending on the plant. Most plants do better in non-sticky soil, although you should check to see what soil is best for your plant.

When you repot your plant, remember to mix in nutrients for growth, and pumice or gravel for drainage.

Frequently asked questions about light

Why do my plant's leaves look pale or discoloured?

Sometimes leaf discolouration can be caused by a lack of water or too much water. Sometimes leaves will change colour because of nutrients in the soil. But oftentimes, leaves will change colour because of a change in light intensity. In nature, when the seasons change, so does the light intensity. Plants typically adjust how much light their leaves take in by changing colours.

What is the best type of light for plants?

All light is good for plants, but different plants prefer varying degrees of light intensity. Wanderers and plants that come from shaded regions might prefer less light than plants from bright regions.

While sunlight is one of the best sources of light for plants, they can also use light from light bulbs in your home for photosynthesis.

Frequently asked questions about watering plants

How do I know if I have overwatered my plant?

Your plant's leaves and stems will tell you. If the leaves become droopy and sticky, this means that you have overwatered your plant. The base of the stem will also show signs of root rot if it becomes flimsy and brown.

Is it enough to just water the base of the plant?

Always water where the roots are. If all the roots are contained in the soil, then water the soil thoroughly. If your plant has aerial roots or roots along the stem, make sure to spray these roots with water, and explore using paper towels or a moss stick to encourage these roots to grow and help your plant become longer.

If you have a vine with aerial roots but you don't want it to grow longer, it is okay to just water the roots in the soil.

After repotting and watering my plant, the soil sinks. Should we refill the soil in the sunken area or just leave it?

If the soil sinks when you water your plant, it is because you did not push the soil down when you first potted the plant, leaving air gaps between layers of soil. When you water soil that hasn't been pressed down, the air pockets fill with water and the soil sinks down.

If you notice the soil sink more than a centimetre, wait a few days for the top layer of soil to dry, and then add another layer of soil. Gently push the soil down to fill in any air pockets. Remember to keep a few centimetres of empty space at the top of the pot so that water doesn't overflow when you water your plants.

I advise people to fill the sunken area because you had a vision for how high you wanted the soil, but maybe forgot to press it down. Now that the soil has been compacted, it is okay to add a little more soil to reach the desired level you originally intended.

How do I know if the roots are rotten?

Rotten roots are typically sticky while normal roots are coarse and dry, even after being watered. Sometimes, if you are worried that there is water sitting in the soil, it is okay to try to repot it. Just be careful not to lift it out of the pot. Instead, loosen the soil around the edges of the pot with a khurpi, then put your hand over the top of the pot, flip it and let the plant slide out. Letting the plant slide out instead of pulling the plant ensures that you do not tear the roots. When you have the plant out of the pot, you can examine the roots, and move it to dry soil. Make sure the new pot has a good drainage system (holes at the bottom of the pot and a layer of gravel.)

Another sign of root rot is if the base of the stem seems brown, weak and flimsy. But typically, by the time the rot reaches the stem, it is too late to save the plant, although you may be able to take a cutting and propagate a new plant.

What temperature should the water be that I use to water my plants?

Always use room temperature water. If the water is too cold or too hot, it could shock the roots of your plants, affecting their growth and their ability to take in water. If you're worried that the water is too hot or cold, you can let it sit out in your room for an hour until it reaches a neutral temperature.

Frequently asked questions about soil

How often should we aerate or till the soil?

I recommend tilling the soil for aeration every one or two months, or whenever you notice the soil is compact. Only till the soil when it is dry; tilling wet soil can close off air passageways. Also, use an appropriately-sized tool. If your khurpi is too big for the pot, you are more likely to cut and damage the roots. We also want to till the soil right before monsoon season or before a heavy rain. It is a good idea to aerate the soil before watering to help the water drain evenly. Remember—be careful not to cut the roots!

What do I do if the soil in a pot is hard?

If the soil has hardened within the pot to the point where you are unable to till it, you can remove the soil mass from the pot and attempt to break the soil into chunks. I recommend using your fingers to knead the soil so you don't damage the roots.

Once you break up the soil into smaller particles, you can repot it, or mix in a more loamy or fine soil.

To prevent the soil from hardening again, make sure to till it on a regular basis, especially before you water it. Always water the soil thoroughly and evenly so that one area does not become clumped up with water, else it will harden that way and become difficult to break up, till and aerate. It's good to mix pumice stone into the soil to promote even drainage and prevent the soil from hardening.

Frequently asked questions about nutrients

How often should I add fertilizer to my pot?

It depends on the type of fertilizer, the current season and your plant's needs. Most fertilizer is either slow-release or fast-release. Fast-release is best to use on seeds or when plants are just sprouting, while slow-release is best to use on plants once they have matured. Many slow-release fertilizers, or fertilizer sticks, should be reapplied every couple of months. Fast-release fertilizers typically need to be reapplied every couple of weeks. It is okay to add nutrients to your soil if you notice signs that your plant may be lacking nutrients such as discoloured leaves or stagnant growth.

Frequently asked questions about what your plants' leaves are trying to tell you

What does it mean if a plant's leaves have yellow or brown tips?

Leaves with yellow or brown tips are a sign of stress that can be caused by the following factors:

- Underwatering
- Overwatering
- Sunburn

Why do the tips of my spider plant become dry?

If your plant's leaves have dry tips, it usually means that the plant is too hot or needs more water. If it is only the tips that become dry during the summertime, it may not be a problem, especially if no other part of your plant seems affected. It is common for plants to become a little dry and brown at the tips during the summer. If the dryness expands beyond the tips of the leaves to the rest of your plant, move your plant into partial shade or a cooler area.

What do I do if my plant's leaves turn white?

If your plant's leaves turn white, it could be a sign of variegation, which is a rare phenomenon where the plant's pigment is altered. In most cases, variegation is fine for the plant. In fact, many gardeners seek out variegated plants, so if your plant does have stark white areas on its leaves, you may want to keep watching it and propagate it to see if you can create more variegation.

If the leaves are more of a pale yellow colour, almost white, then it is probably a sign that it lacks nutrients, needs water, has been overwatered or is unhappy with its temperature.

Keep an eye on your plant. If you notice more leaves turning pale yellow, look for signs that it needs water or has been overwatered, and follow the instructions in the previous chapters.

What do I do if my plant has mealybugs?

Mealybugs are tiny little white bugs that look like a powder when grouped on your plants. These bugs will quickly eat your plant, including its roots, which can kill the plant. Mealybugs also enjoy sucking the juice out of plants, so they are often drawn to storage houses. Mealybugs will also attract ants that like to eat the honeydew that mealybugs secrete.

If you notice mealybugs on your plants, spray your plant with a mild soap solution in the evening and wash it off in the morning. Repeat three or four times over a period of four weeks.

What do I do if my plant is infested by pests?

Pests can be a general nuisance to plants, eating them, attracting other pests and killing your plant over time. If you notice pests on your plant or plants, do the following:

- Move any plants with pests away from other plants. I highly recommend moving any plants with pests outside so they do not infest your home.

- Identify the pests. Online research can be very helpful.
- You will most likely need to repot and remove all pests
- For some pests, there may be a natural solution or pesticide. Just because a pesticide is natural doesn't mean it's harmless.

If you use a pesticide, **read the caution label and keep away from kids and pets.** Many pesticides include volatile organic compounds, so never eat or drink any of these solutions, and be careful not to get them in your eyes. I recommend wearing gloves. Look for a lower rating pesticide if you can help it.

Frequently asked questions about repotting

How do I know when to move my money plant into a larger pot?

Money plants, along with other wanderers, do not need to be moved to a larger pot because they are easy to propagate. Instead of repotting my money plant, I personally prefer to take a cutting and start a new pot of money plants. If you would rather your original money plant grow bigger, you can nurture the aerial roots using a moss stick or napkins.

You can repot your money plant into a larger pot, but it is not the easiest way to get a bigger money plant. It is difficult to move a money plant attached to a moss stick because separating the moss stick from the vine would mean tearing away the aerial roots and damaging the plant. If you do move a money plant while it is attached to a moss stick, it is important to break the pot and carefully move the entire plant into a larger pot of soil while it is attached to the moss stick.

How often do I need to change the moss stick for wanderers?

You do not need to change the moss stick. The purpose of the moss stick is to provide moisture to the aerial roots. Some gardeners recommend changing the moss stick every five years. But how do you change the moss stick when the roots are already attached to it? In my experience, you can use the same moss stick for the life of the plant.

What do I do if my plant becomes wilted after repotting?

Plants often wilt when their roots are unable to absorb water. If you just repotted your plant, there are a few reasons why the roots might stop absorbing water:

1) The soil is too compact
2) The roots may have been destroyed when repotting
3) The roots have rotted from too much moisture

I first recommend using a khurpi or flat tool to till and loosen the soil. Be gentle and careful not to disturb the roots.

If your plant is limp near the stem, then it most likely has root rot, which is difficult to fix. If your plant can be propagated, you can try to propagate a new plant using a cutting.

Always be careful not to pull or tug when repotting your plant. I always say to flip the plant and let it slide out of the pot so that we don't accidentally ruin the root system.

Does the soil need to be dry when repotting?

Yes. It is better and easier to repot with dry soil. If the soil is wet, it behaves more like clay and will become too compact. Sometimes the soil may seem too dry. It is okay if there is a little bit of moisture in it. So if the soil feels too dry to push down, sprinkle just a few millilitres of water on it.

Is it okay to use thalamocele or marbles instead of gravel to filter water at the bottom of the pot?

Technically, yes. Remember, the purpose of the gravel is to prevent the hole or holes at the bottom of the pot from being clogged by soil as you water your plant. You can use any solid material that isn't porous or affected by water, meaning it doesn't compact when it becomes wet. Make sure that whatever you use is larger than the hole so that it doesn't fall through. Also, avoid using any materials made of aluminium or other metals that can leach into the soil and harm your plant. I find that rocks and gravel work best.

Another option is to take a net and spread it at the bottom of your pot to prevent gravel from falling through if the hole is larger than the pieces of gravel you are using.

I repotted my plant and all the leaves have withered. There are no signs of new growth. How long should I wait for my plant to show signs of new growth?

Unless you notice sure signs that there is a problem such as root rot or pests, I recommend being patient for at least a few months. I have brought plants back to life that seemed dead, so it is possible. Plants move very slowly, and sometimes even become dormant during winter or if they feel shocked. Plants like bougainvillea can take months to show new growth after old leaves wither away.

Be patient but keep an eye on the plant and the soil. Make sure that it is still getting water after the soil has completely dried out. Also, make sure that it is not too cold or too warm, and that you keep it in the right light conditions. If your plant was healthy before you repotted it, chances are it is stressed, but it will recover.

How do I repot a plant that has been overwatered?

First, remove the plant from the old pot by loosening the soil around the edges and flipping the pot. If there is still a lot of moisture in the soil, you may need to spend extra time loosening the soil and tap the bottom of the pot gently. Be prepared to hold the plant with your other hand so that it doesn't fall on the ground.

Once the plant, roots and soil are out of the old pot, I recommend leaving it on a tray or in a larger pot (without adding new soil) so that it has extra time to dry out. Trim away any roots that look infected or rotted. Roots should be firm and white. If they are soft and coloured brown or black, then they are infected and should be cut to prevent the infection from spreading further. If the primary root looks rotted, you will have to cut off the entire root system and attempt to propagate the plant.

If you are worried that you overwatered your plant, I would first move it to brighter light instead of immediately repotting it.

Instead of changing pots, can I trim the roots and keep my plant in the same-sized pot?

Yes, you can take your plant out of the pot, trim the roots back and put it back in the same pot. Your plant will stay the same size, but it will still be happy in the old pot. Just don't cut away the primary root.

This concept is the same as bonsai in Japanese culture, but you can apply it to any plant. In bonsai, the plant is usually kept in a shallow pot, and the branches are trimmed to resemble a smaller version of larger trees found in nature.

If you want the plant to grow bigger, you will eventually need to move it to a bigger pot to give the roots more room to grow.

How do I repot a plant with multiple stems, like ZZ plants, peace lilies or aglaonema?

To repot plants with multiple stems, follow the same process of loosening the soil and flipping the plant, using your other hand to catch the plant as it slides out of the pot. After removing the plant, you have the option to either plant all the stems in a larger pot, or separate each stem and plant them in separate pots. If you do separate the plant, be careful not to disrupt the primary roots coming down from each stem. You may have to untangle secondary and tertiary roots, sometimes even using bypass pruners to cut away at the small roots.

If you do separate the plants, you may want to put them in the same-sized pots since they are now two smaller plants. You can also add other plants and cuttings to the pot to create an arrangement of plants like a bouquet or terrarium.

Can I repot my plant into a pot that already has plants in it?

Yes, it is okay to have multiple plants in the same pot if it is big enough to hold all the plants. I still advise waiting at least a week from when you bring your plant home before repotting, and to be careful not to disturb the roots of the plants already in the pot when making space for your new plant. You may have several plants of same type or even several different types of plants in a single pot. If you are planting different types of plant in a single pot, make sure all of them have similar light, water and nutrition requirements.

Are we supposed to cover the drainage hole when repotting the plant?

We never want to completely cover the drainage hole(s) at the bottom of the pot. When we add a layer of gravel, it should not block the hole. Instead, the layer of gravel should prevent the soil from spilling down and clogging the hole when it is wet. The water should have a clear path for easy drainage.

Is it okay to use a pot with no drainage hole?

No. There should always be a hole at the bottom of the pot to allow water to drain. You can try to drill a hole in the pot yourself, but depending on the material of the pot, it may be difficult. If you do make your own hole, do it when the pot is empty so you don't accidentally damage the roots.

The only time it is okay to use a pot without holes is as a cache pot, or a decorative outer pot. In this case, the plant should still be in a pot with a drainage hole, and then that pot can be placed inside of the larger pot with no hole. Whenever you water your plant, take the inner pot out of the decorative pot, water until it drains from the bottom, let it dry for a little while, and then place it back in the decorative pot.

I'm worried about pushing down the soil when I repot my plant. How do I know I'm not damaging the roots?

Always use your fingers to press the soil down and be gentle. We don't want to apply so much force that we squish the roots. One thing I like to do is spread my fingers so that the pressure is evenly distributed over the soil, and I'm not pushing down in one area. Also, make sure that you're pushing down the soil around the plant, not the plant itself. Your fingers should be at least a centimetre or two away from the stem of the plant itself.

If you're worried, chances are you're going to be careful. Roots can be delicate, but they can also survive a little bit of pressure and weight. If they couldn't, they would have a difficult time surviving underneath the soil.

Don't shy away from pushing the soil down. Air gaps are not good for your plant's roots. It is always better to fill in the air gaps with a little push because air pockets will cause the plant to lean and prevent the roots from absorbing the nutrients and water they need to grow and be healthy.

Helpful Plant Lists

Reasons to garden

- Plants make us happy.
- Plants look amazing.
- Plants quiet our busy minds.
- Plants teach us patience.
- Plants make us feel at home.
- Plants bring people together.
- Plants make life possible.

Plant myths

- 'I do not have a green thumb.'
- 'People who travel can't keep plants.'
- 'Plants bring bugs inside.'
- 'Plants will kill me in my sleep.'
- 'Plants improve indoor air quality.'
- 'Plants need to be outside.'

- 'Water is always the answer.'
- 'Expensive means better.'

Best plants for new gardeners

- Coleus
- Pothos
- Aloe-vera
- Snake plant
- ZZ plant
- Syngonium
- Song of India
- Areca Palm
- Croton
- Philodendron

New gardener's toolkit

- Khurpi
- Gardening mat
- Soil scoop
- Pots and planters
- Soil
- Coco peat
- Plant food
- Watering can
- Pumice stone

Low-light plants that do well indoors

- Aglaonema
- Begonia

- Cast iron plant
- Dumb cane
- Peace lily
- Philodendron heartleaf
- Pothos
- Snake plant
- Spider plant
- Syngonium
- ZZ plant

Plants that like bright, indirect light

- Alocasia
- Calathea
- English ivy
- Ferns
- Fiddle leaf fig
- Kentia palm
- Monstera
- Peperomia
- Raphis palm
- Rubber tree plant
- Song of India

Plants that like bright, direct light

- Aloe vera
- Any flowering plant
- Areca palm
- Bougainvillea
- Cactus

- Croton
- Devil's backbone
- Herbs such as rosemary, mint, thyme, sage, lemongrass, oregano
- Ponytail palm
- Rhoeo
- Sago palm
- String of pearls
- Succulents
- Tulsi

Plants that are toxic to dogs and cats

- Aglaonema
- Aloe vera
- Asparagus fern
- Devil's ivy
- Dracaena
- Jade plant
- Peace lily
- Philodendron
- Pothos
- Sago palm
- Snake plant

Plants to keep on your bright, sunny balcony

- Aloe vera
- Areca palm
- Bird of paradise plant

- Coleus
- Croton
- Hibiscus
- Monstera
- Rubber plant
- Snake plant
- Succulents
- ZZ plant

Plants that can be air layered

- Almost all stiff and sterns
- Bougainvillea
- Croton
- Fruit trees such as mango, lemon, lychee, custard apple, guava and pomegranate
- Hibiscus
- Jasmine
- Neem tree
- Rose plant
- Rubber plant

Plants that can self-propagate

- Aloe vera
- Dracaena
- Pilea
- Snake plant
- Spider plant
- ZZ plant

Plants that can be propagated with a leaf

- Cactus
- Jade plant
- Kalanchoe
- Peperomia
- Snake plant (Sansevieria)
- Sedum
- Succulents
- ZZ plant

Plants that can be propagated in water

- Aglaonema
- Almost all wanderers
- Begonia
- Coleus
- Croton
- English ivy
- Fiddle leaf fig
- Lucky bamboo
- Mint
- Monstera
- Peace lily
- Peperomia
- Philodendron
- Pilea
- Pothos
- Prayer plant
- Rhoeo
- Rosemary

- Rubber tree plant
- Snake plant
- Spider plant
- Succulents
- Syngonium
- Wandering Jew
- ZZ plant

Plants that prefer red soil

- Red is rich in iron oxide, lime and aluminum. Vegetables that grow best in slightly acidic souls (pH of 6.0–6.5) would be leafy greens, peas and beets, also radishes and sweet potatoes, citrus trees, tomatoes, etc.

Plants that need to be handled carefully

- Aloe vera
- Alocasia
- Any ficus
- Any thorny plants
- Devil's backbone
- Dumb cane
- English ivy
- Ferns
- Jade
- Monstera
- Peace lily
- Philodendron
- Poinsettia
- Pothos

- Sago palm
- Weeping fig
- ZZ plant

Common pests

- Aphids
- Gnats
- Mealybugs
- Slugs
- Snails
- Spider mites

Fun plant-growing exercises for kids

- Rooting an onion
- Rooting and growing a carrot top
- Rooting celery
- Growing microgreens
- Germinating rajma
- Growing a citrus tree
- Turning almost anything into a pot
- Making a water bottle vertical garden

Afterword

A Time to Be Lazy and a Time to Get to Work

I sincerely thank you for taking the time to read my book about gardening. I hope the information, stories, tips and words of wisdom have been and will continue to be useful to you in your journey as a plant parent, gardener and advocate for the natural world.

I know I like to joke and call myself the 'lazy' gardener. I do believe that taking care of plants should be a move-at-your-own speed practice. If anything, plants teach us how to slow down rather than always feel like we need to be active. They teach us how to stop and appreciate our senses in the moment: the smells of flowers, the beautiful colours and shapes of the leaves, the different textures of each leaf and stem of a plant. When I call myself lazy, I mean taking the time we need to appreciate the beauty all around us. Moving slow and taking it all in will naturally make you a happier, healthier person who wants to make the world a better place.

At the same time, I believe that plants teach us how to be responsible. When we garden, we move more slowly, but we also become more aware of how we live in harmony (or disharmony) with nature and one another. If we are not careful, we may destroy nature faster than it has time to grow. We cannot force growth, either. We simply have to take the time and care to nurture our world.

I believe that when I learn something significant to our well-being and the well-being of others, it is worth sharing. I encourage you to introduce someone else in your life to plants, whether by giving them a cutting, letting them borrow this book or even inviting them to enjoy some of the plants you are growing.

If we all spread the joy and lessons plants teach us, I truly believe we can preserve the natural beauty of our world for generations of gardeners to come.

—Vinayak Garg

Acknowledgements

This book would have never been created if it were not for the support and feedback of the plant parents across India who joined the Lazy Gardener community. Their active participation in my workshops and social media posts helped me get a better understanding of what plant parents need and gave me a nudge to encapsulate it in this book. I have to start by thanking each and everyone who follows Lazy Gardener on Instagram, Facebook, YouTube or LinkedIn, and each and every customer of Lazy Gardener.

The team at Lazy Gardener has been a huge support to me. There have been many people who have helped shape my social media content over the years and to experiment with workshop structures. I want to thank Kopal Nanda who helped me structure the offline plant parent meetups (pre-pandemic) and ideate on the book much before I wrote the first words. Pallavi Gupta has been a tremendous help in every content that I have put out—she has acted as an objective critic, and is the sole reason why I have continued to experiment with my content.

Neha Iyer helped me stay sane through the two years journey of the book, by helping me make tough decisions and taking care of all challenges relating to this book.

I am eternally grateful to my mother and father for raising me with plants and to my sister for sharing wonderful childhood memories—which have shaped me into the person that I am today.

A very special thanks to my friend Phalguna Kommareddy, whose encouragement is the only reason I began Lazy Gardener. He continues to be a constant support and critic of everything I do.

Gurveen Chadha, my publisher at Penguin deserves special thanks—her constant push to move from one step to the next has allowed the book to see the light of day. It has taken two years for this book to move from the first chapter to print, but without her push, it would have been a decade. Thank you Tejas Modak for being patient and incorporating numerous changes in the illustrations.

Finally, to all those who have been a part of my getting there: Manoj Kathuria, Simran Kaur, Satwik Kommareddy, Harpreet Dhingra, Sunaina, Anshika Bhandari, Nandini, Yatu Bui, Tathagat Mukherjee, Aman Mishra, Shailesh, Ashish, Piyush Bansal, Mithuram, Apurva Yadav, Shweta Kalyankar, Swati Dang, Bhawna Ahuja, Manisha Yadav and Anish Malik for this. The Lazy Gardener team who enables me to be the founder of a company that I'm honoured to be a part of, thank you for letting me serve, for being a part of our amazing company, and for showing up every day and helping me take care of the operational aspects of running a company.